Spar-Torpedo Instructions for the United States Navy

United States Naval Torpedo Station (Newport, R.I.)
Foreword by Jellicoe [AI]
Enhanced by Nimble Books AI

Nimble Books LLC

Publishing Information

(c) 2023 Nimble Books LLC
ISBN: 9781608882595

Algorithmically Generated Keywords

ship torpedo spar; torpedo outfit supplied; contact spar leading-wires; service torpedo; ship secondary spar; plate xvi; dry gun-cotton primers; contact torpedo; pattern; chemical box; wire box; permanent wires; exercise torpedo; machine connecting wires; ends; blocks; boat spars; hand-firing key; torpedo station; circuit; detonator; battery; torpedoes; wet gun-cotton; rubber; testing

Foreword

Since the American Civil War, torpedoes have been an essential part of American naval capabilities, enabling the US Navy to defend and protect American interests at sea. The torpedo, then as now, is the ultimate close-range weapon for sinking ships; a mission that remains essential today.

This book, published in 1890 by the United States Naval Torpedo Station (Newport, R.I.), was a comprehensive guide on how to connect, prime, and test spar torpedoes; fill them with gun-cotton; connect the wires using circuit-closers, and more. Spar torpedoes were attached to a spar on the bow of the ship and meant to detonate on contact with an enemy. Needless to say, the nature of the weapon presupposed that it would be deployed. By bold and skillful seamen.

In this manual readers will discover a detailed overview of torpedo technology as well as helpful instructions for every stage of handling these powerful weapons. The step-by-step approach makes it easy to understand even complex topics like wiring diagrams and primers that may be too confusing otherwise. The US Naval Torpedo Station experts provided their expertise on topics that range from basic torpedo assembly checkout procedures all the way up to intricate explosion mechanisms.

This document reflects well on the technical capabilities of the US Navy at the end of the 19th Century. But it also sheds light on the requirements for naval success at the beginning of the 21st Century. As war machines become more advanced, the knowledge of how to reliably destroy them at close range has retained its importance.

Jellicoe [AI]

Abstracts

TL;DR (One Word)

Contact.

TL;DR (Vanilla)

Connect the torpedoes, prime them, test them, fill with gun-cotton, and connect the wires using a circuit-closer.

Scientific Style

This study presents a method for connecting and priming torpedoes, filling them with gun-cotton, and connecting the wires using a circuit-closer. The efficacy of this method was tested and results showed that it was suitable for constructing torpedoes and can be used in torpedo-based applications.

Explain It To Me Like I'm Five Years Old

A torpedo is like a big metal tube with a special weapon inside it. To make it work, you need to connect it to electricity and make sure it is ready to go. You do this by priming it, which means making sure all the parts are ready to work. Then, you need to test it to make sure everything is working right. After that, you need to fill it with a special type of explosive called gun-cotton. Finally, you need to connect some wires.

Red Team Critique

The document did not specify who should carry out the tasks related to connecting, priming, and testing torpedoes; filling them with gun-cotton; and connecting wires using a circuit-closer. Without identifying the responsible person(s) required to complete the actions outlined in the document, it would have been difficult to ensure that this process is completed efficiently and correctly.

The document also did not provide any safety procedures or guidelines regarding the handling of the explosives contained in the torpedoes, such as protective clothing, respirator masks, and hazard signs. Without this information, workers may have be exposed to potential dangers related to the explosives contained in the torpedoes and the accompanying operator error.

The document does not provide any information regarding the testing mechanism for the torpedoes. It is unclear how the torpedoes are tested for proper operation and if there will be any quality control measures in place to ensure that the torpedoes are functioning properly before being put into use.

Finally, the document does not discuss disposal methods for the explosives after they have been used. It is essential that there be a plan in place for safely and responsibly disposing of the explosives in order to minimize any potential environmental damage or health risks associated with their disposal.

DISSENTING PERSPECTIVE

Just as in 1890, the naval establishment is forcing the US Navy to use outdated torpedo technology. Embracing newer technology could provide an advantage over our opponents, but instead the massive procurement bureaucracy of the DoD status quo stifles everything.

Our traditional approach to torpedo warfare puts us behind other countries who are already relying on cavitating technologies like Russia's Shkval high-speed torpedo. We should prioritize replacing the current Mark 48 with a more powerful alternative.

The constant emphasis on tradition over innovation has hampered our ability to keep up with other nations. Our military hardware must keep pace with our rivals and this document illustrates that we are not doing enough to ensure that.

It is clear that the defense establishment is preventing our forces from getting the best technology available. We must rise up and demand that our soldiers get the equipment they deserve and stop settling for outdated processes such as those outlined in this document.

ACTION ITEMS (1890)

Read and understand the safety instructions for handling torpedoes.

Connect the torpedo to the power source and test it for proper operation. Prime the torpedo with gun-cotton and ensure that it is securely sealed. Connect the wires to the torpedo using a circuit-closer.

ACTION ITEMS (TODAY)

Summarize current US capabilities for close-range anti-ship mission-kill.

Evaluate alternatives to current torpedo technology, such as the drone speedboats flotillas used successfully by Ukraine against Russian targets.

Summaries

Methods

Extractive summaries and synopsis fed into recursive, abstractive summarizing prompt to large language model.

Reduced word count from 19905 to 1 words by extracting the 20 most significant sentences, then looping through that collection in chunks of 3000 tokens each 3 rounds until the number of words in the remaining text fits between the target floor and ceiling. Results are arranged in descending order from initial, largest collection of summaries to final, smallest collection.

Machine-generated and unsupervised; use with caution.

Recursive Summary Round 0

Connect torpedo to terminals of permanent wires, prime Service Torpedo with dry gun-cotton, connect to either boat or ship's spar, test firing battery, do not connect until instructed.

Circuit-closer Pattern B, testing 32 jars, glass for dry primers, knives, lead-covered wires, leading-wires, packing spherical rubber, paper fasteners, permanent wires, pins for circuit-closer spare, plate testing and firing, plates earth, pryers cutting, precautions for gun-cotton inspection, preparation of contact torpedo exercise Pattern D, service Primer blocks.

Inspection & testing of torpedo parts (case, dry gun-cotton, reeving lines, line weights, resistance of detonator bridge, rivets, rubber diaphragms, packing, tubing, washers & safety-pins) with instructions on packing & stowing and precautions to be observed.

Weight, space and stowage of articles 57 Tape, okonite 18, 52 Terminals 15 connection with not to be made until 20 Test circuit through circuit-closer, Pattern B, how to 22, 23 Condition of firing batteries, how to 28, 30 Tester, battery 28, 55 Test, gun-cotton. Testing and firing-plate 53, 56 Circuit-closer, Pattern B 22 Circuit from boat 21 Ship 20 Continuity of wires 32, 38 Detonator circuit in contact torpedoes 24 Manner of 17 When, put in a safe place 17 Gun-cotton articles for insulation of wires 32 Magneto 31, 32, 55 Toggles secondary spar 5, 53 Topping lift ship's spar 16 Torpedo contact circuit-closer to be tested before priming 22 Fusing 23 No connection to be made until 21 Preparation of 22 Priming proper distance and immersion shipping safety-pin to be in splicing on detonator.

Test circuit to fire on contact, sparling leading-wires, pattern B, exercise pattern D, necessary to be water-tight, no connection until number issued, outfit of packed preparation of primer not to remain in long priming, shipping spindle packed, splicing detonator on testing weight, empty of charge when issued filled with wet gun-cotton, proper distance and immersion instructions, copies of outfit. Torpedo service pattern D, splicing detonator on 18" spindle, 2, 55" testing 20, 21" weight empty 2" of charge when issued filled with wet gun-cotton 2, 39, 44" spars, ship's 15" number of 15 Torpedo Station articles supplied from 52" store-room 51 Torpedoes firing using A Machine and firing-key 21" Will.

Connect wires to torpedo using circuit-closer, pattern B 24 Wire box, boat's 7, 54", ship's 6, 7, 53" Wire, continuity of testing 32", 38" insulation of 37" "not to be damaged", 37" testing 32" splice, insulating 38" Wires, contact spar leading, pattern B 7, 22, 23, 24" lead-covered 14" machine connecting 6, 7, 52, 53, 54".

RECURSIVE SUMMARY ROUND 1

Connect torpedo, prime with dry gun-cotton, test firing battery, inspect/test parts, weight, space and stow articles. Test circuit-closer, firing plates, wires, detonators, magnetos. Do not connect until instructed.

Prepare and prime torpedoes with detonator and test circuit, fill with wet gun-cotton, connect wires to torpedo using circuit-closer, pattern B.

RECURSIVE SUMMARY ROUND 2

Connect, prime, and test torpedoes; fill with gun-cotton; connect wires using circuit-closer.[1]

---

[1] This feels like a very effective summary.

Mood

Figure 1.Black and white sketch of spar torpedo attack on British warship in 1890. (herb.loc['ai'] using Stable Diffusion).

Figure 2. Black and white sketch of spar torpedo attack on British warship in 1890. (herb.loc['ai'] using Stable Diffusion).

SPAR-TORPEDO INSTRUCTIONS

FOR THE

UNITED STATES NAVY.

1890.

PREPARED AT THE TORPEDO STATION,

BY DIRECTION OF THE

BUREAU OF ORDNANCE.

TORPEDO STATION PRINT.
MAY 1890.

These Torpedo Instructions, revised and prepared at the Torpedo Station by order of the Bureau of Ordnance, are approved for use in the Navy.

W. M. FOLGER,
Chief of Bureau.

Bureau of Ordnance,
  May 1st, 1890.

LIST OF PLATES.

PLATE.
- I. Service Torpedo.—Pattern D.
- II. Exercise Torpedo.—Pattern D.
- III. Circuit-closer, Contact Torpedo.—Pattern B.
- IV. Fig. 1. Ship's Secondary Spar.—Pattern A.
- " Fig. 2. Boat's Secondary Spar.—Pattern A.
- V. Contact Spar Leading-Wires.—Pattern B.
- VI. Spar-Torpedo Boat-Fittings.—Pattern B.
- VII. Junction of Tubes Forming Boat's Spar.—Pattern A.
- VIII. Fig. 1. Detonator.
- " Fig. 2. Detonator Block.
- IX. Fig. 1. Permanent Wires.
- " Fig. 2. Connections with Firing Key of "A" Machine.
- " Fig. 3. Connections with Firing Battery.
- X. Fig. 1. Electric Switch.
- " Fig. 2. Terminal.
- XI. Heel-Fittings for Ship's Spar.
- XII. Ship's Spar-Fittings.
- XIII. Battery Cell.
- XIV. Battery Tester.
- XV. Fig. 1. Hand-Firing Key.—Pattern B.
- " Fig. 2. Diagram Showing Hand-Firing Key in Circuit.
- XVI. Fig. 1. "A" Machine and Firing Key Connected.
- " Fig. 2. "C" Machine Connected.
- XVII. Fig. 1. Firing Key, Short Circuit.
- " Fig. 2. Firing Key, Testing Circuit.
- " Fig. 3. Firing Key, Firing Circuit.
- XVIII. Steam-Drier.

CONTENTS.

CHAPTER I.
PAGE.

Spar-Torpedo Outfit — General Description — Care and Preservation 1

CHAPTER II.
Preparation of Torpedoes 17

CHAPTER III.
Electrical Apparatus 27

CHAPTER IV.
Gun-Cotton — How Packed — Stowage — Care — Inspection and Drying 39

APPENDIX.
Duties of the Inspector of Ordnance — List of Articles in Outfit — Weights — Stowage Space 51

INDEX 59

PLATES 69

Spar-Torpedo Instructions.

CHAPTER I.

SPAR-TORPEDO OUTFIT.

GENERAL DESCRIPTION.—CARE AND PRESERVATION.

Class D.—Includes one set of Ship's Torpedoes, Service and Exercise, one set of Boat's Torpedoes, Service and Exercise, and one set of circuit-closers and appurtenances for the conversion of Service into Contact Torpedoes.

Service and Exercise Torpedoes are to be used from ships and boats; Contact Torpedoes from boats only.

Many articles in a Torpedo Outfit are common to the different sets comprised in Class D, in which case similar articles are classed together for convenience of stowage and transportation. If the whole of Class D is not issued, then only a proportionate part of those articles designated as "Spare" are issued. Articles that belong exclusively to any one set are issued with that set only.

SERVICE TORPEDO.

Pattern D. — Plate I.

(Twenty-four are issued. — Twelve for use from ships and twelve from boats.)

This torpedo, intended for use from either ships or boats, is $12\frac{3}{8}$ inches long and 9 inches square, inside measurement, and is made of sheet iron tinned inside and out, coated inside with shellac and painted outside with asphaltum. Around a filling hole in the top is soldered a brass ring having on its inner circumference, a screw-thread for a brass screw-cover which bears a stuffing-box for the entrance of the spar leading-wires. A rubber washer between the cover and ring makes the case water-tight. Riveted to the top is a tinned malleable iron frame fitted with four lugs. A handle secured to two of the lugs forms a brace for the spindle that attaches the torpedo to the secondary spar; this spindle has two curved arms at one end that straddle the handle and secure to the other two lugs by screw-bolts, a projection on the crown of the handle fitting into a recess in the stem of the spindle. To the bottom of the case is riveted a tinned malleable iron plate for attaching a circuit-closer.

The primer-case, $8\frac{1}{8}$ inches long and 3 inches square, inside measurement, is made of tin coated inside and out with shellac and is closed at one end.

The torpedo-case, empty but complete except the spindle, weighs about 15 lbs. The charge of the torpedo, including the primer of $2\frac{1}{2}$ lbs. of dry gun-cotton, is equivalent to about 34 lbs. of dry gun-cotton.

When issued, the torpedo-cases are completely filled with wet gun-cotton, the screw-cover is screwed down tight and the hole in the stuffing-box is closed tight by screwing down the water-cap over the spherical rubber packing placed sideways in its seat.

EXERCISE TORPEDO.

Pattern D.—Plate II.

(Twelve are issued, two of which are empty, for use from ships or boats).

This torpedo, $12\frac{1}{2}$ inches long and $3\frac{1}{16}$ inches square, inside measurement, is made of tin and is closed at the lower end. It is coated inside and out with shellac. To the upper end is soldered a brass flange having a loop on one side and a throw-back hinge on the opposite side. The cover consists of a square brass plate with two loops one of which rests over the loop on the flange, the other receiving the lug of the throw-back hinge. A thumb-screw, fitted to the end of the lug, secures one side of the cover and a transportation thumb-screw, fitted to the loops, secures the other side. The cover bears a stuffing-box for the entrance of the spar leading-wires. A rubber washer between the cover and flange makes the case water-tight. A loop is fitted to one side of the case to receive the lower end of the spindle.

The weight of this torpedo, empty but complete, except the spindle, is $3\frac{1}{4}$ lbs. and its charge is equivalent to about 4 lbs. of dry gun-cotton.

When issued, all the exercise torpedo-cases, except two, are completely filled with wet gun-cotton, the cover is closed tight and the hole in the stuffing-box is closed tight by screwing down the water-cap over the spherical rubber packing placed sideways in its seat.

STUFFING—BOXES.

Plates I. and II.

Stuffing-boxes provide a water-tight entrance for the spar leading-wires through the covers of the torpedo-cases.

In the center of each cover, around the hole for the entrance of the leading-wires, is a brass rim fitted with a screw-thread outside, and bored out, inside, with a slightly conical taper, providing a seat for the packing.

The packing is of partly vulcanized rubber, 1 inch in diameter, spherical in shape, with two parallel holes, each $\frac{1}{4}$ inch in diameter, for reeving the leading-wires.

The water-cap screws on the brass rim and compresses

the packing in its seat, a friction-ring in the top of the cap preventing twisting of the packing when screwing down.

A hole, $\tfrac{5}{8}$ inch in diameter, through the top of the water-cap, permits reeving the spar leading-wires.

When rubber packing is to be left seated for a long time the seat for the packing should be coated with shellac and the packing brushed with black lead to prevent adhesion.

CIRCUIT—CLOSER.—CONTACT TORPEDO.

Pattern B.—Plate III.

(Four are issued, to convert Service Torpedoes into Contact Torpedoes, for use from boats.)

The circuit-closer consists of a cylindrical brass casting, having one end closed, and on this end are four feet by which it is secured to the lower head of the service torpedo by screws. The cylinder, $4\tfrac{3}{4}$ inches long and 5 inches in diameter, is closed at the open end by a screw-cover, having four lugs that serve as bearings for the contact-arms; these arms, four in number, work in slots cut in a plunger that passes through the center of the cap, and they are held in place by screws through the ends of two arms and their lugs. Inside the cylinder are two insulated contact-springs secured to binding-posts in an ebonite collar. This collar screws on the end of a short brass tube that carries a plunger tipped on the inner end with ebonite. A stout spiral spring in the tube through which passes this plunger, maintains, normally, the end of the plunger clear of the contact-springs. A rubber diaphragm separates the plunger in the cover from the plunger in the tube, and also acts as a washer to the cover, making the cylinder water-tight; a brass washer, laid on this diaphragm, acts as a friction-plate for the cover to turn on when screwed up. A safety-pin through the outer plunger prevents its being forced in accidentally. When this pin is withdrawn, any pressure on the contact-arms tends to force the inner plunger in against the action of the spiral spring and to close the break between the contact-springs.

The break is $\frac{3}{16}$ inch and the tension of the spiral spring is 75 lbs.

On the side of the cylinder is fitted a stuffing-box furnishing a water-tight entrance for the leading-wires to the binding-posts of the contact-springs.

The circuit-closer, complete, weighs 7 lbs.

SECONDARY SPARS.

Pattern A.—Plate IV.

(One is furnished for each Service Torpedo.)

These are iron pipes, 8 feet long. Those for ships' use have a slot cut in one end, for a key. Those for use in boats are fitted at one end with an iron disc, called a butt, and at 2 feet 2 inches from the butt an iron cap is riveted to the spar. All secondary spars have, at 5 inches from the outer end, a hole for the torpedo-pin. Secondary spars are packed six in a box; those for ships having a key stopped to each to be used in securing the secondary spar to the inner spar-band; those for boats having a toggle stopped to each to be used in securing the secondary spar to the boat spar.

TORPEDO PINS.

Plate IV.

Torpedo pins are short iron pins with an eye in one end, to which a spun-yarn tail is spliced, designed to secure torpedoes to secondary spars. One is provided for each service and exercise torpedo. They are packed, with the spindles, in Box 53.

REEL-BOX.

This contains 300 feet of insulated double-conductor wire cable. The inner ends of the cable are connected to binding-screws on the sides of the reel, where short wires are to be attached, for making connections with batteries, etc., after the requisite amount of cable has been unreeled. A handle is becketed to the cover of the box, to be used in reeling up the cable. The binding-screws must be kept free from rust (no oil to be used in cleaning), and must be occasionally turned to keep them from setting.

The cable, as now issued, consists of two cores, each core composed of seven No. 22 A. W. G. copper wires of not less than 95% conductivity, coated with tin and laid up in a strand. Each core is separately insulated with okonite composition to an external diameter of $\frac{1}{4}$ inch and is wrapped with tape soaked in okonite composition. The two insulated cores, laid side by side, are covered with hemp braiding to protect them from chafe.

The resistance of the core is 2.2 ohms per 1000 feet.

The cable in the reel-box is for general use and to replace disabled permanent wires. It must never be subjected to a strain of over 100 pounds, nor jerked or hauled in from any length, but under-run.

The cable must be stowed in a cool, dry place.

SHIP'S WIRE-BOX.

This box is marked "Wire-Box—Ship's." It contains four spar leading-wires of insulated double-conductor copper wire cable, 70 feet each in length, precisely similar to that found in the reel-box, and two machine-connecting wires 12 feet each in length.

The spar leading-wires are to connect the torpedo with the terminals of the permanent wires. To guard against mistakes in making connections those for use on the starboard side are painted green and marked with one knot and those for use on the port side are painted red and marked with two knots.

The machine-connecting wires are insulated wires for connecting the D. E. machine, Pattern A., with the firing-key and for general purposes.

BOAT'S WIRE-BOX.

This box is marked "Wire-Box — Boat's." It contains the same articles as "Wire-Box — Ship's," similarly marked.

CONTACT SPAR LEADING-WIRES.
Pattern B. — Plate V.

These consist, practically, of three insulated copper wire cables which lead, in use, as follows:— 1st. wire, from the detonator to one terminal of the battery; 2nd. wire, from the circuit-closer to the second terminal of the battery *via* the safety-break; 3rd. wire, branching in two legs at its outer end, from the detonator and the circuit-closer to the second terminal of the battery *via* the hand-firing key and the safety-break.

The safety-break and the hand-firing key are connected to their proper leads by wires of convenient length to permit placing the battery out of the way when connected up.

The safety-break consists of two round, tapering pieces of brass each fitted with a score and two small holes in the smaller end to which the leading-wire is permanently secured. The larger ends, fitted to ship together bayonet fashion, can be readily connected or disconnected at pleasure.

Directions for using these wires are given in "Preparation of Contact Torpedo."

SPAR—BANDS.

Plate IV.

These, of wrought iron, furnish a ready means of securing secondary spars to the ordinary wooden torpedo-spars supplied to ships. These bands, with loops on top, are secured to the end of the wood spar, 3 feet apart, with wood-screws. The inner band has a key-way, to hold the secondary spar in place. Care must be taken that the loops of both bands are exactly in line.

SUPPLY—BOX.

This box, containing tools and small articles required in spar-torpedo work, is marked on top, "Torpedo Supply-Box." For contents see Box 3 "List of Articles in Outfit supplied from Torpedo Station."

BOAT—FITTINGS.

Pattern B.—Plate VI.

These, for the support and handling of the boat spars, consist of bow-fittings, 2 swivel-crutches and 2 heel-rests.

The heel-rest is an iron crutch bolted to the rail well aft. A hinge allows the rest to be laid inboard when not in use.

The swivel-crutch is a square iron collar fitted with a shank that turns freely in a bearing firmly bolted to the rail, 9 feet abaft the cross-beam. The collar is made in two parts, the upper one working on a hinge, and has two rollers.

Bow-fittings consist of a cross-beam with its attachments. The cross-beam, made of heavy wrought-iron tubing, is secured across the bow to castings let into the rail. On sleeves, at the ends of the cross-beam, are elevating-arms free to revolve in a vertical plane. At the outer end of each arm a swivelled guide-ring is placed, projecting at right angles to the arm in the direction of the beam of the boat. In the lower part of this ring is a roller. Connected with the sleeve of each arm is a gear moved by a worm on the forward end of a shaft extending aft into the boat, an elevating-wheel being keyed to the after end of the shaft.

The worm-shaft is in two lengths joined by a hook-coupling interposed near the forward end of the shaft to allow the worm sufficient play to engage the gear of the elevating-arm during the revolution of the shaft.

The worm-shaft is allowed a fore-and-aft motion such that, when the shaft is forward, the worm is disengaged from the gear of the elevating-arm, leaving it unsupported and free to drop and, when the shaft is aft, the worm is engaged with the gear so that the elevating-arm may be controlled by the elevating-wheel.

The shaft is held aft by a clutch placed just forward of the elevating-wheel. The clutch consists of a sleeve, supported on trunnions by a bearing bolted to a chock on the forward deck of the boat, carrying a yoke-link, loosely bolted to two lugs on its forward lower end and a detaching-lever, loosely bolted to two lugs on its forward upper end. The worm-shaft, passing through this sleeve, bears a rigid collar so placed that, when the shaft is aft, the collar is close up against the forward end of the sleeve. The yoke-link, when swung up, embraces the shaft and bears against the forward side of the collar, holding the shaft aft. The yoke-link is held up by the detaching-lever which is thrown forward between the upper ends of the yoke-link, a transverse roller in the detaching-lever, with ends projecting on either side, locking the yoke-link in place. A pin, passed through eyes worked in the upper ends of the yoke-link, prevents accidental tripping of the detaching-lever. When this pin is withdrawn and the detaching-lever is pulled aft the yoke-link falls and the shaft is free to move forward.

By the worm-shaft and its attachments the elevating-arm can be rotated around the cross-beam, held in any position in its plane of rotation, or released at any desired moment.

The gear and worm are protected by hoods.

BOAT SPARS.

Pattern A.—Plate VII.

The spar, made of steel, consists of two tubes, 18 and 15 feet long respectively, one 4 inches and the other $3\frac{1}{2}$ inches in diameter, joined together with a telescopic joint. The tubes—with a lap of 2 feet—are held together by two screws. At the larger end of the spar is an eye-bolt for the heel-rope screwed in from the inside, and at 5 feet from the smaller end is a hole for reeving the spar leading-wires. This constitutes the main spar, which can readily be taken apart for stowage by removing the screws. To assemble the spar, a feather fits into a score on the end of the larger tube, bringing the screw-holes opposite each other. Iron spar-clamps are furnished, to facilitate the assembling of the spar.

The two tubes composing each spar are marked by similar letters or numbers.

Note.—Spars must invariably be taken apart after use, joints lubricated, and protected by a canvas cover.

DETONATORS.

Plate VIII.

Detonators are cylindrical copper cases, closed at the bottom, containing 35 grains of fulminate of mercury, primed on top with dry, pulvurulent gun-cotton.

A plug, made of 1 part of ground glass and 2 parts of sulphur, melted together, is cast around the detonator-legs:— tinned copper wires, No. 20 A. W. G., 6 inches in length, insulated with a double layer of cotton thread soaked in paraffine, the outer layer colored red.

The inner ends of the detonator-legs are bridged by a platinum-iridium wire, 90% platinum, 10% iridium, $\frac{8}{16}$ inch long and 2 mils in diameter, having a resistance of $.65 \pm .03$ ohm.

The plug is inserted in a copper band; dry pulvurulent gun-cotton is loosely packed about the bridge and on top of the fulminate of mercury and the band is screwed on the upper end of the detonator-case, thus closing it.

Detonators are painted red. They are supplied for use with gun-cotton torpedoes.

DETONATOR BLOCKS.

Plate VIII.

Wooden cylinders, with a cover that has a small circular motion. Each block holds 8 detonators placed in holes around the circumference, the cover locking them in. Each block is placed in a covered tin cylinder painted red and marked "Dangerous." These blocks will be placed in different parts of the ship, never below the water-line. (See Ord. Inst.)

DUMMY DETONATORS.

These are empty detonator-cases, with a hole bored in the bottom, for use in making connections in practice. The detonator-legs are not bridged but are cast in the plug on the bight.

Dummy detonators are painted white and the legs are insulated with white cotton thread.

IGNITERS.

Igniters are cylindrical brass cases, closed at the lower end, containing a charge of rifle gun-powder.

The upper end is closed by inserting a plug precisely similar to that used in detonators, except that the igniter-legs are insulated with white cotton thread instead of red.

The bridge is primed by twining about it a wisp of long-staple, dry gun-cotton.

Igniters are coated with white shellac. They are supplied for use with improvised gun-powder torpedoes.

GUN—POWDER FUZES.

These are stout, cylindrical, paper cases, closed at the lower end and charged with rifle gun-powder. In the center of the charge is placed an igniter the legs of which project on either side of a wooden plug which is seized in the upper end of the case to close it.

Igniters are coated with orange shellac.

A rubber insulator, for preventing short-circuit between the splices when the fuze is attached to leading-wires, is seized around the upper end of the case.

Fuzes are supplied for use with improvised gun-powder torpedoes.

BOX CONTAINING GUN—POWDER FUZES AND IGNITERS.

This is marked with a list of contents. It is packed in Box 7, from which it is to be removed, when received aboard ship, and stowed in the magazine or ammunition room.

GLASS JARS FOR DRY PRIMERS.
Pattern B.

Glass cylindrical jars, fitted with cork covers, each having a capacity for 6 two-inch, or 24 one-half inch blocks of gun-cotton. These blocks of dry gun-cotton are tied together with boiled tape and have litmus-paper between them. They are never to be stowed below, but must be placed in different parts of the ship above the water-line. Being glass, the jar, without being opened, renders the litmus-paper readily discernible. Each jar is placed in a wooden case fitted with a sliding cover, painted white, and is stencilled with contents, and with precautions.

The dry primers, as used, are replaced by drying the wet blocks removed from the torpedoes in priming them.

GUN—COTTON DRYING APPARATUS.

Plate XVIII.

A steam-drier, for drying wet gun-cotton for use as primers, consists of a sheet-iron box containing two removable galvanized-iron wire baskets in which the blocks to be dried are supported, strung on rods. The blocks are separated from each other by small iron washers, $\frac{1}{4}$ inch thick, also strung on the rods, to permit free circulation of the air. A door in the front of the box permits entering and withdrawing the baskets.

In the bottom of the box is a flat of steam-pipe the two ends of which, projecting from the side, are screw-threaded for ready connection with steam-heating apparatus, or with any other convenient source of low-pressure steam.

A wire-gauze bottom, below the flat of steam-pipe, permits the entrance of air and serves to keep out dust and to prevent undue radiation of heat toward the outside.

In the top of the box is a ventilating opening, with a rotary damper, protected by a hood, and also a hole for the introduction of a thermometer.

CHEMICAL BOX.

This box is marked on top "Chemical Box." For contents see Box 16, "List of Articles in Outfit supplied from

Torpedo Station." For use of contents see "Inspection of Gun-Cotton."

The outfit includes a number of spare washers, spherical packings, diaphragms, etc., to supply necessary waste.

In addition to the articles already mentioned, every vessel having a "Ship's and Boat's" spar-torpedo outfit is supplied from the Torpedo Station with the following articles, to be placed on board at the navy-yards, as permanent fittings; viz.:

Double-conductor insulated copper wire, incased in lead, in such quantity as may be required for permanent wires; 2 electric switches; 13 terminal binding-screws.

PERMANENT WIRES.
Plate IX.

In order to do away with the inconvenience of leading out lengths of wire from place to place, and to avoid injury to the wire, permanent wires are put in place when the ship is fitted out. These wires are led from terminals conveniently placed for battery connections *via* the electric switches or firing apparatus to the terminals, abreast the heels of the torpedo spars.

Permanent wires should be protected from hostile fire, from chafe, wear, and the sun; should never be taut; should never be led around sharp angles; metal staples should never be used to hold the wires in position, even temporarily; no part of the copper wire should be exposed to the action of salt water; splices should be soldered and carefully insulated; and the wires should be boxed in throughout their lengths.

ELECTRIC SWITCHES.
Plate X.

In connection with permanent wires electric switches are used, and are permanently placed in a suitable position before a ship leaves the navy-yard.

Their object is to connect the firing-battery or the firing-key of the D. E. machine with any or all the torpedoes. The plate represents the switch in position, on the starboard side, with the battery off, or the wires from the firing-key disconnected from any permanent wire, electrically. The switch should be protected from salt water and the weather as much as possible. It is thought best to inclose it in a box, as nearly water-tight as possible, provided with a door which opens in front.

Note.—Where permanent firing apparatus is furnished, the electric switches will not be issued.

TERMINALS.
Plate X.

Terminals are ordinary brass binding-screws secured to base-pieces of black walnut which are to be secured in position by screws. The figure illustrates the manner of making permanent and temporary connections with the terminals. The counter-sunk space in the back of the base-piece is to be filled with melted wax, after the permanent wire has been attached, before securing the terminal in place. The binding-screws must be kept clean and free from paint.

ARTICLES OF TORPEDO OUTFIT SUPPLIED AT NAVY-YARDS.

Ship's Spars.—Such ship-rigged vessels as are now fitted for spar-torpedoes are supplied with four torpedo-spars, fitted two on each side, abreast the foremast and mizzenmast. Barque-rigged vessels are supplied with but two spars, fitted one abreast the foremast on each side.

The present regulation spar is of hickory or oak, 45 feet long, 8 inches in diameter at the heel, and 6 inches at the outer end. It should be of the best material, straight-grained, and as nearly as possible a natural-growth pole. In working down a larger spar, care should be observed to follow the grain of the wood. Yellow oak is considered superior for torpedo-spars. Red oak is too brash.

The Heel Fittings. (*Plate XI.*)—The thrust-plate is placed at about the height of the channels, in accordance with the regulations established by the Bureau of Ordnance. Discretion must be used in so placing this as to allow the spar to come alongside, so that the torpedo can be shipped from the rail or from a port. The elbow of the heel-bolt transmits the recoil of the spar to the thrust-plate, without injury to the bolt itself. Good results have been obtained by using a lashing of 6 turns of $3\frac{1}{2}$-inch manilla, in place of the shackle, the elasticity of the rope serving to take up a portion of the thrust of the spar. An excellent plan is to secure the heel of the spar to a spare eye-bolt in the channels, as shown in Fig. 2.

The Spar Fittings. (*Plate XII.*)—The most approved method of fitting a torpedo-spar with guys and topping-lift is shown in the plate. Spans are fitted to the spar on which the forward guy and topping-lift travel freely, and these spans are rove through lizards to divide the strain along the spar and prevent vibrations. The forward guy should be single, with as much drift as possible, and long enough to let the spar trail aft, after the explosion. The forward guy, the pendant of the topping-lift, or that part of it secured to the span, the spans and lizards should be of galvanized-iron wire rope, $\frac{5}{8}$ inch in diameter. The after guy may be a single part of small manilla rope, say 3-inch. The forward guy should be led from as near the water-line as possible to keep the spar from rising.

CHAPTER II.

PREPARATION OF TORPEDOES.

SERVICE TORPEDO.

Pattern D.—Plate I.

Priming the Service Torpedo.—Take the torpedo out of its box; remove the screw-cover of the case and take out the wet gun-cotton found in the primer-case; wipe the primer-case dry and insert a primer of 16 one-half inch blocks, or 4 two-inch blocks of dry gun-cotton.

The wet gun-cotton removed from the primer-case is to be put in one of the empty exercise torpedo cases and dried when opportunity offers.

Wipe the screw-thread carefully and screw down tight the cover on its washer, taking care not to cut it, using the open-end wrench provided for the purpose in the supply box. *It is absolutely necessary that this case be closed water-tight.*

Note.—It is not advisable to prime torpedoes for a much longer time before using than the exigencies of the service require, although experiments at the Torpedo Station show that service gun-cotton torpedoes may remain primed for three months, under service conditions, and yet be relied upon to explode.

Testing the Detonator.—Select a detonator, brighten the ends of its legs and attach them to leading-wires. *Put the detonator in a safe place,* connect the leading-wires to the terminals of the testing-magneto and turn the crank. Rattling of the armature will indicate continuity of the circuit and is presumptive evidence that the detonator is good. The wires from the detonator can be taken to the binding-posts T, T of the firing-key of the A machine and tested, a deflection of the needle furnishing proof of continuity (*Plate XVI*); or they can be taken to the terminals of the C machine which will indicate continuity by the striking of its gong. (*Plate XVI*).

Splicing on the Detonator. (*Plates I and II.*)—The detonator should now be spliced to the spar leading-wires. In splicing on the detonator, so arrange the length of wire that the spherical rubber packing can be placed on the leading-wires five inches from the bottom of the detonator-case, the splices being between the detonator and the packing. Remove the water-cap from the screw-cover of the case. Strip the braiding and rubber tape from the leading-wires for at least six inches from their ends and put on a neat whipping, which shall be outside the packing.

Reeve the ends of the leading-wires through the water-cap and rubber packing. Remove so much of the insulation as may be necessary, for making the splice, from the leading-wires and from the legs of the detonator; brighten the wires and place the insulation of the detonator-legs alongside that of the leading-wires, with the ends of the insulation flush, and expend the bare detonator-legs in turns at right angles around the leading-wires. Turn the ends of the leading-wires back over the splices, and trim off the ends. *One splice should be one-half inch from the detonator and the other one inch from the packing.* Insulate from metallic contact the splice nearest the packing with twine and pass several turns about the wires until the detonator is reached, where the end of the twine is secured. A strip of okonite tape can be used, taking care that the insulation is not to bulky. (See sample splice in supply-box).

Fuzing the Service Torpedo. (*Plate I.*)—Having lined the holes of the dry blocks with the rectifier, to be found in the supply box, enter the detonator through the hole in the cover and push it in until the packing is seated; screw up the water-cap hand-tight. Provide the spindle, to be found in Box 53, and secure it to the torpedo-case.

Shipping the Secondary Spar. (*Ship's.*)—Enter the end of the secondary spar in the loop of the outer band, and push in until the key-way is abreast the slot in the loop of the inner band; then put in the key and stop it in.

Shipping the Service Torpedo. (*Ship's.*)—Insert the stem of the spindle in the outer end of the secondary spar and push it home as far as the shoulder. Put in the torpedo-pin and stop it in.

To prevent the strain of towing from starting the splice, turn a cuckold's-neck in the spar leading-wires, and lash it to the secondary spar or to the spindle, clear of the torpedo-case. The spar leading-wires should then be led in along the ship's spar, abaft the topping lift, and stopped to it at intervals of about four feet.

Fuzing and Shipping the Service Torpedo, and Shipping the Secondary Spar. (*Boat's.*) **Pattern B. Boat-Fittings.**—See that the elevating-arm points aft. Rig in the main spar clear of the guide-ring. Point the inner end of the secondary spar through the guide-ring, the outer end resting on the rail. Reeve the leading-wires through the guide-ring from forward aft, and fuze the torpedo. Then ship the torpedo in the secondary spar, securing it by the torpedo-pin, which must be stopped in. Turn a cuckold's-neck in the leading-wires and stop it to the secondary spar or to the spindle, clear of the torpedo-case. Slue the secondary spar in position, butt aft. Reverse the elevating-arm, by revolving it downward, until the guide-ring is in line with the swivel-crutch and heel-rest, carefully tending the inner end of the secondary spar by a line bent on. Ship the secondary spar in the main spar, by rigging the latter out or in, and secure it by a toggle, which must be stopped in.

The boat spar leading-wires are rove through the main spar. To facilitate this, a reeving-line and weight, found in the supply-box, is rove through the main spar, before the secondary spar is shipped; one end of the line is secured to the heel-bolt, and the other around the spar abreast the wire-hole.

When the secondary spar is shipped, bend the end of the leading-wires to the reeving-line, rig out the torpedo until the heel of the spar is conveniently placed for hauling on the after end of the reeving-line, and reeve the leading-wires through the spar, being careful to avoid chafing the insulation.

When the contact spar leading-wires are used they must be rove through the main spar, from aft forward, before fuzing the torpedo.

The spar leading-wires from the heel of the ship's spar are taken to the terminals abreast the heel of the spar; from the heel of the boat's spar they are taken directly to the C machine, or to the firing-battery, a hand-firing key being interposed when the battery is used. (*See Plate XV.*)

No connection, however, is to be made with terminal, machine, or battery, until the torpedo is submerged and at the proper distance from the side of the ship or boat.

Testing the Circuit from Ships.—After the torpedo is submerged the circuit may be tested, to do which connect the spar leading-wires to their proper terminals and connect the binding-screws T, T, of the firing-key, to the proper permanent wires. Place the firing-key as directed for testing the detonator, ship the crank of the D. E. machine, turn rapidly with the sun, and press the key T of the firing-key. A deflection of the compass needle will indicate that the circuit is complete. (*See Plate XVI.*) Or, the testing-magneto may be used to test the circuit.

The firing-battery must not be used to test the circuit.

To Fire.—Make connections with the firing-battery, or with the A machine (*Plate IX*). When using the battery, close the hand-firing key at the moment it is desired to fire. When using the A machine, press the key F of the firing-key, and keep it down; turn the crank of the machine rapidly, and at the instant it is desired to fire, press firmly the key T of the firing-key (the key F being already down).

The Service Torpedo must be immersed 10 feet, and from ships may be safely exploded at 35 feet from the side.

To Test the Circuit from Boats.—The spar leading-wires are brought directly to the machine, (*See Plate XVI*), *but not connected until the torpedo is submerged*, when the circuit may be tested by connecting it to the binding-screws of the C machine, turning the crank of the machine and pressing the key T, as for testing the detonator. Or, the testing-magneto may be used to test the circuit.

The firing-battery must not be used to test the circuit.

To Fire.—Make connection with the battery (*Plate XV*), or with the C machine (*Plate XVI.*) When using the battery, close the hand-firing key at the desired instant. When using the C machine, manipulate the keys as directed for the firing-key of the A machine.

The Service Torpedo must be immersed not less than 10 feet, and may be safely exploded at a horizontal distance of 22 feet from the boat.

EXERCISE TORPEDO.

Pattern D.—Plate II.

Priming the Exercise Torpedo.—Remove the transportation thumb-screw and loosen the thumb-screw on the lug of the hinge. Throw back the cover, replace the second wet block of gun-cotton from the top with a dry 2-inch block, or four $\frac{1}{2}$-inch blocks, and put the cover back in place; insert the spindle, to be found in box 53, through the loops on one side and screw down taut against its shoulder; screw down also the thumb-screw on the lug of the hinge. *It is absolutely necessary that this case be closed water-tight.*

The wet gun-cotton removed is to be placed in one of the empty exercise torpedo-cases, to be dried when opportunity offers.

Note.—Do not allow the dry primer to remain in the exercise torpedo any considerable length of time before use, as it may absorb enough moisture to prevent detonation.

The detonator is tested and spliced, and the torpedo fuzed in the same manner as directed for the Service Torpedo.

Shipping the Exercise Torpedo.—To be done in the same manner as prescribed for the Service Torpedo.

The Exercise Torpedo may be used from either a boat's or ship's spar. It may be safely exploded at an immersion of 5 feet, and a horizontal distance of 20 feet.

PREPARATION OF THE CONTACT TORPEDO.

Pattern D.—Plate V.

To Convert a Service Torpedo into a Contact Torpedo.—Attach a circuit-closer, Pattern B, to the frame on the lower head of the torpedo by screws through the lugs.

Testing the Circuit-Closer.—Remove the water-cap and spherical rubber packing from the side of the circuit-closer; remove its screw-cover; take out the inner plunger. Remove the braid for a few inches from the longer leg (insulated double-conductor cable) at the outer end of the contact spar leading-wires, whipping the braid. Remove the rubber tape from the conductors, and pass them through the water-cap and packing and through the cylinder of the circuit-closer. Remove the insulation for one inch, brighten and lay up the naked wires and connect them to the binding-posts of the circuit-closer, taking care that the bare ends do not project far beyond the binding-posts. Seat the inner plunger, hauling on the wires at the same time, so as not to leave any slack wire in the cylinder. Set down the water-cap on the packing in the side of the circuit-closer. Replace the diaphragm, friction-plate and screw-cover. Remove the insulation for one inch from the shorter legs at the outer end of the leading-wires, and bend the naked wires together temporarily. Connect the inner ends of the leading-wires with the terminals of the testing-magneto, or of the C machine. Close the safety-break. Remove the safety-pin from the circuit-closer and press down the contact-arms. Under these circumstances a test with the testing-magneto, or with the C machine should show continuity. Release the contact-arms and put in the safety-pin. A test should now show no continuity. After this test the safety-pin must not be removed until just before submerging the torpedo prior to firing.

It is absolutely necessary that the circuit-closer be closed water-tight.

Priming the Contact Torpedo.—Proceed as in priming the Service Torpedo.

Fuzing and Shipping the Contact Torpedo, and Shipping the Secondary Spar.—Proceed as with the Service Torpedo, except that the contact spar leading-wires must be rove through the main spar, from aft forward, before fuzing the torpedo. The detonator must be spliced to the short legs of the leading-wires.

To Test the Circuit.—The torpedo having been submerged, connect the inner ends of the leading-wires to the testing-magneto, or to the C machine. Close the safety-break and the hand-firing key and test. Under these circumstances continuity should be found.

To Fire at Will.—Connect to the firing-battery, close the safety-break and, at the desired moment, close the hand-firing key.

To Fire on Contact.—Connect to the firing-battery. Close the safety-break. When contact is made the contact-arms will be forced in, and the torpedo will explode.

Note.—The safety-break should be habitually left open, being closed only just before it is desired to put the circuit in condition to fire by closing either one of the two remaining breaks—that in the hand-firing key, when firing at will, or that in the circuit-closer, when firing on contact.

IMPROVISED TORPEDOES.

Torpedoes may be readily improvised from kegs or casks pitched outside. The fuze should be put in place before filling with powder, in order that it may be near the center of the charge. The spar leading-wires pass out through the close fitting scores in the bung. The latter, after being secured in its place, should be pitched over thoroughly, and weight added to the whole, in order that it may be readily immersed. For exercise torpedoes, bottles, oil-cans, etc., may be used.

An excellent composition for rendering the bung and the entrance of the leading-wires water-tight is made by melting together 8 parts of pitch, 1 of beeswax and 1 of tallow. It is to be applied while fluid.

In order to burn all of the powder in the torpedo, a spindle, to contain the fuze, should be made on board of wood, following the general form of spindle in a gunpowder torpedo, and using a wrapping of cotton cloth, bunting, or paper, to prevent the powder passing through the flame-holes and choking up the spindle.

Splicing on the Fuze.—To splice the fuze to the spar leading-wires so arrange the length of wire that the fuze will be entered in the spindle, reaching well into the torpedo-case when the entrance for the wires is closed. The leading-wires must be stripped of covering exterior to the insulation, to a distance extending to just outside the entrance. At this point the outer wrapping on the wires should be secured by a good whipping. If the outer wrapping on the wire is admitted inside, it will, after a time, act so as to introduce water to the charge.

To make the splices, strip the insulation from the leading-wires for about an inch, and brighten them. Brighten the fuze-legs and twist them around the leading-wires in a manner similar to that employed in the Service Torpedo, arranging the splices, however, so that they shall be at equal distances from the top of the fuze. Cut off extra ends and lay the splices in the scores of the fuze-plug; turn the insulator down over them, and secure it with the insulator fastener. (See sample splice in supply-box).

USE OF THE PERMANENT WIRES AND ELECTRIC SWITCHES.

Connecting. (*Plate IX.*)—The connections with the firing-battery are as follows:—one wire from each switch is connected to one battery terminal, and the common-return wire, with the hand-firing key interposed, is connected to the other battery terminal.

The connections with the firing-key of the A machine

are as follows:— one wire from each switch is connected to one binding-post, marked T, of the firing-key, and the common-return wire is connected to the other binding-post of the firing-key, also marked T.

When electric switches are used an intelligent and careful person must be stationed at each switch, the index of which must be kept pointing toward "Battery off; connection through," except when it is desired to prepare the circuit for firing any torpedo, when the index must be turned so as to point toward the torpedo which is about to be fired.

The circuit for firing any single torpedo may thus be arranged; or, by moving the index to point toward "Battery on both" the circuits will be prepared for firing the two attached to that switch.

By a proper manipulation of the switches the circuits may be prepared so that any one, two, or three, or all four of the torpedoes may be fired simultaneously.

It must be borne in mind, however, that the electric switch is only a commutator for establishing the paths of the currents and that it must not be used as a firing-key.

CHAPTER III.

ELECTRICAL APPARATUS.

FIRING—BATTERIES.

Voltaic batteries are supplied for firing torpedoes from ships and boats. A modification of the Le Clanche' cell has been adopted and is now issued from the Torpedo Station. One ship's firing-battery of six cells is supplied to such ships as are fitted with spars. For use in boats and elsewhere, as may be necessary, two boat's firing-batteries of four cells each, with two spare cells for each battery, are supplied. When the guns are to be fired by electricity an additional firing-battery will be furnished for the purpose.

Note.—Ships having only one torpedo launch will be supplied with but one boat's battery.

THE CELL.

Plate XIII.

The positive element is zinc in the shape of a cylinder open at both ends. Around the zinc is molded a covering of okonite, which forms the jar of the cell. A lug from the zinc cylinder projects up through the okonite covering and has soldered to it the brass negative terminal of the cell. The negative element is a thin plate of platinum enclosed in a cylindrical muslin bag filled with crushed carbon. The bottom of the bag is closed by a flat, circular piece of ebonite. The top of the bag is seized to a plug of ebonite, through which passes a platinum wire, soldered to the platinum plate and to the brass positive terminal in the top. The ebonite plug is scored to take a rubber cover, the outer edge of which fits in a groove cut around the inside of the okonite cylinder above the top of the zinc, preventing loss of the liquid by splashing, or by evaporation. A hole in the cover permits the entrance of air, which is necessary for the proper operation of the cell. A rubber ring around the lower end of the negative element prevents its contact with the zinc. The liquid is a nearly saturated solution of sal-ammoniac (ammonium chloride). This cell polarizes rapidly on a short-circuit, but recovers in a few hours if left on open circuit.

FIRING—BATTERY FOR SHIPS.

The ship's firing-battery consists of six cells inclosed in a box. The cells are joined up in series. The terminals are at one end of the box, on top, and are covered by a lid hinged to the cover of the box.

FIRING—BATTERY FOR BOATS.

This pattern is similar to the ship's battery, except that four cells only are inclosed in its box.

BATTERY TESTER.
Plate XIV.

This consists of a small wooden case inclosing a resistance-coil and a fuze-bridge. One end of the coil is connected to a brass spring and the other to one end of the fuze-bridge; the other end of the fuze-bridge is connected to a brass contact-piece opposite a spring at the other end of the case. When the tester is laid over the terminals of the battery and pressed down, contact is made between the contact-piece and spring, and a circuit established through the resistance-coil and bridge. If the battery is in good condition the bridge will be seen to redden, through a glass plate in the top of the case. The resistance of the coil in the tester for the ship's battery is 6.5 ohms and in the tester for the boat's battery it is 4 ohms.

Should the fine wire bridge accidentally be broken, the plug must be removed and a new one inserted. A number of plugs, with bridges, are supplied for this purpose.

MANAGEMENT AND CARE OF FIRING—BATTERIES.

To Prepare the Liquid.—Make a saturated solution of sal-ammoniac with rain or distilled water. The solution will be hastened by crushing the crystals of sal-ammoniac and heating the water. Allow the solution to cool and settle, and decant it carefully. Then add one-tenth its volume of distilled or rain water.

One pound of sal-ammoniac to four pints of water will give the proper degree of saturation.

To Fill the Cells.—Press down the edge of the rubber cover at one point and, by inserting a screw-driver at this point, pry up the cover, and lift its edge all around. Introduce the liquid through a glass funnel, being careful to spill none of it on the connections, and fill the jars to within half an inch of the top. After twenty-four hours replenish the liquid, filling the jars to the same point as before, and replace the rubber cover.

The ship's battery should be kept in a locker provided for it on the berth-deck, and should be kept connected with the wires leading to the firing-apparatus on the spar-deck.

Neither the ship's nor the boat's firing-batteries are to be tested too frequently, nor must the duration of a test be longer than is necessary. The batteries, if kept stationary in a proper locker, need be tested but once weekly. The boat's battery must be tested before it is sent into the boat, and again after it is put in place in the boat.

The liquid should last from six to twelve months, according to the work done by the battery. Should the battery fail to show the proper test, search for bad or corroded connections. Test each cell separately, by touching the legs of a fuze-bridge directly to the poles of the cell. A single cell should redden the fuze-bridge when no other resistance is interposed. Faulty cells must be taken out, emptied and supplied with fresh liquid.

The batteries must be examined daily. The connections must be kept clean and free from salts and, to secure this, the liquid must not be allowed to come in contact with them. Corroded connections can be cleaned with emery cloth, or, if very badly corroded, they may be scraped with the back of a knife-blade.

Boat's batteries must be habitually examined after use in boats and any liquid that may have splashed about them be carefully wiped off.

It sometimes happens that, from long use and impoverishment of the liquid, crystals of zinc-ammonium-chloride form in the cell, attaching themselves to the muslin bag and to the zinc. Sometimes these crystals build across from the bag to the zinc and prevent the ready removal of the negative element. When this occurs no effort should be made to remove it by force, for such a proceeding is liable to brake the platinum wire, or tear the thin platinum plate. To remove the negative element, take off the rubber cover and pour out the liquid, which should not be used again. Fill the cell with warm water and allow it to stand, full of water, for several hours. The crystals are but slightly soluble, but prolonged soaking will detach them sufficiently to permit the removal of the negative element. When this can be done the crystals are to be carefully picked off the muslin and scraped off the zinc. If such crystals are found in a cell, at any time, they must at once be removed and the liquid renewed.

These batteries require but little care, but this little they must have. Systematic attention to them will be well repaid by their good performance and their constant readiness for use.

Before the firing-batteries are returned into store at the end of the cruise, or before transportation to distant points, the negative elements must be removed from the cells, thoroughly soaked in fresh water and dried. The jars must be washed out and drained and all metal parts wiped perfectly dry.

HAND–FIRING KEY.

Pattern B.—Plate XV.

This consists of two pieces of hickory, shaped to fit the hand, and joined together at the smaller end. Each piece is fitted with a brass contact stud projecting from its inner face at a short distance from the larger end. The natural spring of the wood keeps the two parts separated and maintains, normally, a break between the studs. A hole, bored longitudinally in each part, permits the entrance of a leading-wire, the bared end of which is secured by a screw to the contact stud. A rubber cot is seized over the key to prevent the closing of the circuit by sea-water. A safety-pin, attached to the key by a laniard, is habitually kept between the two parts to prevent accidental closing.

The hand-firing key, introduced in an electrical circuit, provides a break that can be closed at will.

THE TESTING–MAGNETO.

This is a small magneto-electric machine, sending alternating currents into the external circuit. The circuit from the magneto includes an electro-magnet with a vibrating armature.

The magneto will actuate this armature vigorously as a sounder, or rattler, through about 1000 ohms resistance. It may be used for testing the continuity of torpedo and other circuits, or for testing the insulation of the permanent and other leading-wires.

For Testing Continuity.—The poles of the magneto are connected with the ends of the circuit to be tested and the crank turned. If the armature rattles it indicates a continuous circuit. The failure of the armature to rattle will show a break in the circuit.

For Testing the Insulation of the Permanent Wires.—Connect one pole of the magneto with the wire to be tested and the other pole to earth; or, if a cross with some other wire is suspected, the other pole is connected with that wire. If the armature rattles vigorously when the crank is turned, a leak of less than about 1000 ohms resistance is indicated; if not, the insulation resistance of the wire is about 1000 ohms.

To Test the Insulation of a Leading-Wire.—Attach one end of it to one pole of the magneto, the other pole of which is connected by a short length of wire to an earth-plate placed in a tub of sea-water. Keeping the two ends of the wire to be tested out and dry, pay it into the tub gradually, turning the crank of the magneto meanwhile. Should there be a fault in the insulation, its existance and locality will be indicated by rattling of the armature when it reaches the water.

FARMER'S DYNAMO ELECTRIC MACHINE, PATTERN A, AND FIRING—KEY.

Plate XVI.

For a full description of the electric machine, see "A

Lecture on Galvanic Batteries, Part III" published by the Bureau of Ordnance, 1875.

In general, pattern A may be considered as having an electro-motive force of sixteen to eighteen volts and a resistance of five ohms and to be capable of firing from twenty to twenty-five detonators arranged in series, or five to six arranged in as many branch circuits, or a single detonator through $1\frac{1}{2}$ miles of cable such as is now issued, or through twenty ohms resistance.

It is unnecessary to give more than three or four turns of the crank in order to generate sufficient current to fire; but these revolutions must be with the sun and continuous up to and including the moment of firing. In general, as more work is required from the machine, greater speed and longer time will be necessary to get the machine up to its maximum power; this time, however, is very limited and the rapid turning of the crank for half a minute may be considered sufficient. With a single detonator in circuit and a moderate amount of leading-wire, one-quarter of a turn of the crank will usually be sufficient to fire.

Testing the Machine.—To test the machine, connect the binding-screws by a piece of metal, ship the crank and turn it with the sun. If it turn hard the machine is in good order; if it turn as easily as before the binding-screws were connected the machine is out of order.

In case the machine is out of order it should be removed from the outer case and the cause sought out and remedied. There are no delicate parts or mechanism and the machine may be examined without fear of injury.

The only faults which have been observed are the collecting of dirt between the shells of the commutator and the commutator springs, want of contact between them and the collecting of metallic dust between the two shells of the commutator. Each of these faults may be remedied in a moment. It is proper to say that these faults have never occured when the machines were turned by hand and seldom when turned by power at a high rate of speed.

Some of the wire connections inside the machine might be severed by the breaking of a soldered joint, of which there are five. A fault of this kind would be readily found and easily remedied. In soldering electrical connections, resin, and not acid, should be used.

The effect of any of these faults is to cause a break in the continuity of the electrical circuit of the machine. This circuit is as follows: starting from one binding-screw, a wire leads to the field-of-force coils, or electro-magnet coils, traverses them and passes to one of the commutator springs; thence to one shell of the commutator; thence to the coil around the armature, through this coil to the other shell of the commutator; thence to the other commutator spring and, by a wire, to the second binding-screw, thus forming a complete circuit, when the binding-screws are joined together. If they are left unconnected, there is no closed circuit, no current is generated and the armature, therefore, turns easily. When the circuit is closed by connecting the terminals by a conductor of not too great resistance, the current generated excites the electro-magnets and this leads, in turn, to the generation of a stronger current until a maximum is reached depending on the resistance of the circuit and the speed with which the crank is turned. The electrical energy thus developed when the circuit is closed requires, of course, that extra work should be done to turn the crank. When the circuit is broken, inside or outside of the machine, it is necessary to overcome only the friction of the machine and the armature, therefore, turns easily.

The Purpose of the Firing-Key. (*Plate XVI.*)—The

full power of the electro-magnets of the D. E. machine will be reached soonest and will be greatest when the two binding-screws are joined by a piece of metal of practically no resistance as, for instance, a short wire. If this short-circuit is kept closed until the moment of firing and is at that moment replaced by the circuit containing the detonator, we will have the machine working with its magnets fully excited in the circuit in which useful work is to be done. In order to accomplish this change of circuit, without allowing the magnetism of the machine to fall, the second circuit must be completed before the first is broken. If we had no more convenient method we could take advantage of this property of the machine by connecting the two ends of the fuze-circuit to the two binding-screws of the machine, and laying a piece of metal across the two binding-screws. When the crank is turned a strong current is generated, the magnets reach their full strength and, on removing the piece of metal, the machine is thrown upon the fuze-circuit with its magnets strongly excited, generating sufficient current to fire the detonator.

The firing-key furnishes a convenient method for making this change of circuit and also a means for testing the continuity of the fuze-circuit at any time before firing. When the firing-key is connected to the machine by wires between the binding-screws of the latter and those marked B, B, of the former and the binding-screws, marked T, T, of the former, are joined by a wire, there are three circuits which may be closed or broken by manipulation of the keys T and F of the firing-key. (*Plate XVI.*)

The Short-Circuit.—The current follows the path shown in Fig. 1.

The Test-Circuit.—When the key T is pressed, the

short-circuit is broken and the current follows the path shown in Fig. 2.

The Firing-Circuit.—When the keys F and T are pressed, the current follows the path shown in Fig. 3.

To Test the Firing-Key.—Connect as above and place the firing-key about ten or twelve feet from the machine, and so that the compass-needle points in the direction of the length of the box; ship the crank and turn it rapidly; if it turn hard the short-circuit is in good condition; then press the key T; if the crank turn easily and the compass-needle be deflected, the test-circuit is complete; then press the key F (the key T being already down); if the crank turn hard and the needle be no longer deflected, the firing-circuit is complete.

FARMER'S DYNAMO—ELECTRIC MACHINE.

Pattern C.—Plate XVI.

This machine, intended for use in boats, has less power than the large machine, and may generally be considered as having an electro-motive force of eight volts, and a resistance of four ohms, and to be capable of firing eight to ten detonators in series, or two to three arranged in as many branches, or a single detonator through 1500 feet of such cable as is now issued.

This pattern combines within itself the firing and testing apparatus,—that is, the firing-key is permanently connected to the machine and the binding-screws of the C machine occupy a position analogous to that of the binding-screws T, T, of the firing-key.

To Test the Machine.—Ship the crank and turn it rapidly with the sun; if it turn somewhat hard the short-circuit is complete; press the key T; the crank should turn with ease; connect the binding-screws by a short wire; turn the crank as before and press the key T; if the crank turn easier and a small bell be heard to strike inside, the test-circuit is complete. Continue turning the crank, press the key F and then the key T; if it continue to turn somewhat hard, and the bell does not sound, the firing-circuit is complete. The difference of force necessary to turn the crank during the several tests is not so apparent as with the larger machine. If any of the tests fail the machine should be taken from its case and the fault treated as with the larger machines.

WIRES.

Insulation.—Insulation is for the purpose of confining the electric current to the path we wish it to take and should be carefully looked after at all points not covered by the rubber or other permanent insulating matter. Faults in the insulation of the wires leading from the testing or firing apparatus to the torpedo may be so situated as to cause, in the former case, false tests and, in the latter, a sufficient weakening of the current through the detonator to prevent its firing; or, they may be so situated as to cause accidental explosion of the torpedo. The insulation of the wires, as well as that of the testing or firing apparatus, must therefore be carefully preserved.

In order to preserve good insulation, all binding-screws should be kept clean and dry. Rain-water has little effect, but salt-water is bad. Wires which make short angles should be protected from chafe and all splices should be very carefully insulated by rubber tubing.

Particular care must be taken to prevent metallic contact of the two legs of the detonator. Any such contact at that point would not be detected by testing and would be fatal to success.

Splicing Wires.—Remove the jute braiding and rubber tape from the two ends to be spliced for such a distance as to be clear of the rubber tubing used to insulate the splices and whip the braiding. Bare the conductors of the two wires for about an inch and a half, lay them up and brighten them. Slip the piece of rubber tubing over the end of one of the wires. Unite the wires by a square-knot or sheet-bend, soldering the splice if it is to be permanent. Slip the rubber tubing over the splice so that its ends will overlap the rubber insulation of the wires and pass a snug seizing around each end of it.

If the splice is to be permanent a better junction may be made as follows: Prepare the wires as before, bend up slightly the two ends, lay them side by side, and bind them tightly together with a whipping of fine wire; then turn the ends back on the splice and solder the whole together. Another good joint may be made as follows: Prepare the wires, but allow a greater length; lay them together and twist each about the other at right angles and in opposite directions; then solder all together.

In all cases trim the splices so that there shall be no projecting wires to cut through the insulation.

Continuity.—It is possible that a wire may be cut or broken at some point where such cut or break cannot be seen. If there be any reason to suspect such a break, the continuity of that wire may be readily tested by connecting it to the testing-magneto, using leading-wires known to be good, and proceeding as in other testing.

CHAPTER IV.

GUN-COTTON.—HOW PACKED.—STOWAGE.—CARE.—INSPECTION AND DRYING.

PACKING AND STOWAGE OF WET GUN-COTTON.

Each Service Torpedo, completely filled with wet gun-cotton, is packed in a rough box for transportation and stowage. The Exercise Torpedoes, ten filled with wet gun-cotton and two empty, are packed six in a box.

Each filled torpedo has attached to its case a tag on which is marked the gross weight of the torpedo in pounds and ounces, the initials of the Superintendent of the Gun-cotton Factory and the factory number of the charge from which the contained gun-cotton is taken.

When received on board ship the cover on which the address is marked is to be reversed. The torpedoes are then stowed in the magazine in a manner similar to that now employed in stowing shells.

MARKS ON BOXES.

PAT. D. TORPEDO, SERVICE. =....LBS. DRY G. C. *(Factory No. of Charge.)*	PAT. D. TORPEDOES, EXERCISE. =....LBS. DRY G. C. *(Factory No. of Charge.)*

PACKING AND STOWAGE OF DRY GUN-COTTON.

The glass jars for dry primers, filled with dry gun-cotton, are put in wooden cases, painted white, fitted with sliding covers as described on p. 13. The cases are marked "DRY GUN–COTTON PRIMERS. NOT TO GO BELOW." They are packed in a rough box for transportation.

When received on board ship the cases containing the jars are placed in different parts of the ship, but are never to be stowed below the water-line.

On account of insurance restrictions imposed on freight companies it is often impracticable to ship gun-cotton in its dry state. When this is the case the gun-cotton primers are issued wet and are packed in the spare exercise torpedo cases from which, on receipt aboard ship, they are to be removed and dried and then stowed in the glass jars for dry primers.

A Torpedo Outfit, consisting of 24 Service, Pattern D. Torpedoes, 12 Exercise (10 filled, 2 empty), Pattern D. Torpedoes and 4 jars of dry gun-cotton for primers will contain, approximately, the following amount of gun-cotton:—

WET GUN–COTTON.

24 Service Pattern D, Torpedoes $= \begin{cases} 1296\ 2\text{-inch blocks; or } 1200 \\ 2\text{-inch blocks and } 384 \\ \tfrac{1}{2}\text{-inch blocks} \end{cases}$ wet $= 818.1$ lbs. dry.

12 Exercise (10 full, 2 empty) Pattern D, Torpedoes $= \begin{cases} 60\ 2\text{-inch blocks; or } 50 \\ 2\text{-inch blocks and } 40 \\ \tfrac{1}{2}\text{-inch blocks} \end{cases}$ wet $= 37.9$ lbs. dry.

Total wet gun-cotton $= \begin{cases} 1356\ 2\text{-inch blocks; or } 1250 \\ 2\text{-inch blocks and } 424 \\ \tfrac{1}{2}\text{-inch blocks} \end{cases}$ wet $= 856$ lbs. dry.

DRY PRIMERS.

6 each of $\begin{cases} 16\ \tfrac{1}{2}\text{-inch blocks;} \\ \text{or } 4\ 2\text{-inch blocks} \end{cases} = \begin{cases} 96\ \tfrac{1}{2}\text{-inch blocks;} \\ \text{or } 24\ 2\text{-inch blocks} \end{cases}$ dry $= 15.2$ lbs. dry.

Total equivalent of dry gun-cotton in outfit................871.2 lbs. dry.

The wet charge of a torpedo, Pattern D, is composed of blocks two inches thick. The primer charge is composed of blocks $\frac{1}{2}$ inch thick, if there be any on hand; otherwise, of blocks 2 inches thick.

The 2-inch block contains 10.1 oz. and the $\frac{1}{2}$-inch block 2.5 + oz. of dry gun-cotton.

CARE OF GUN–COTTON AND DETONATORS.

The Gun-Cotton Magazine must not be located near the boilers or engines, nor where the temperature of the magazine will equal 105° F. for any great length of time. The magazine should be aired frequently. Avoid as much as possible exposing any box or case containing gun-cotton, dry or wet, to the direct rays of the sun for any length of time, as the temperature inside the box can, in this way, be raised to a point considerably above that of the open air and this temperature will be maintained for a considerable time after the exposure.

The diurnal changes of temperature will not affect gun-cotton, wet or dry, provided that the cases or boxes containing the gun-cotton are not exposed to the sun.

The detonating charges of dry gun-cotton are designated "primers," and the fulminate of mercury igniter as the "detonator."

The primers of dry gun-cotton supplied to each ship are packed in glass jars with tight covers to exclude moisture. Strips of blue litmus-paper are placed between the blocks of dry gun-cotton.

The glass jars will be kept in their wooden cases. The jars and cases are a part of the permanent outfit and must be cared for and returned. Dry gun-cotton is never to be stowed below the water-line, but it may be carried under any deck above the water-line, care being taken that the glass jars, in their wooden cases, are not within 10 feet of each other, nor in the vicinity of the galley or other fires, nor in the immediate vicinity of the guns of the battery.

In removing from their cases the glass jars holding the dry gun-cotton never expose them to the sun, as the glass may act as a lens and cause the ignition of the gun-cotton.

All other primers will be furnished wet, and packed in the torpedo cases.

As the stock of dry primers becomes reduced, a suitable time and place will be selected for replenishing the stock, by drying, according to the rules for drying gun-cotton, the blocks removed from the torpedoes in priming them.

The detonator has a charge of 35 grains of fulminate of mercury. Detonators are placed in circular wooden blocks, bored to hold eight each, each block being put in a tin box. These tin boxes should never be put below the water-line, but kept in a dry place on the upper decks, and not in the immediate vicinity of the galley or other fires, of the battery, or of other explosives. *All loaded detonators are painted red,* and the tin boxes containing them are also painted red and marked on top "DANGEROUS." Great care should be taken to grasp the box by the bottom when lifting or carrying it for, if held by the top only, the bottom, with its block, may slip out.

INSPECTION OF GUN-COTTON.

Weekly — all dry gun-cotton.
Monthly — all dry gun-cotton.
Quarterly — all wet gun-cotton.

INSPECTION OF DRY GUN-COTTON.

Weekly Inspection. — *The dry gun-cotton primers must be inspected weekly.* This can be done without opening the jars, by observing the condition of the blocks and the strips of blue litmus-paper placed between them.

In the event of any serious decomposition having taken

place, the gun-cotton will be found more or less covered with pasty, yellow spots, the jar will be filled with brownish red, highly acid fumes and the litmus-paper will show a decided red color. In this event the gun-cotton may be thrown overboard, but even when in this extreme condition there appears to be little danger of immediate explosion and, if desired for use, this gun-cotton may be wet with the alkaline solution (p. 45), until it has increased 30% in weight, and used as wet gun-cotton. No serious risk will attend this operation. No gun-cotton should be thrown overboard except when a board of experts has pronounced it to be in the condition above described. This is essential, as considerable valuable gun-cotton has been condemned and destroyed and a sense of insecurity has arisen in consequence of errors in inspection.

It frequently occurs that the blue litmus-paper becomes faded by exposure in the jars, but no danger is to be apprehended in consequence.

If the litmus-paper has become reddened, but no fumes or pasty spots are observed, the blocks should be lifted out by the loose ends of the tape and placed on a perfectly clean, dry piece of blotting-paper. Then untie the tape and separate the blocks, being careful not to touch them with the fingers. (A perfectly clean, dry crash towel may be used in handling the blocks.) Remove the strips of litmus-paper, insert freshly moistened strips in their places and tie the tape as before. After an hour's interval examine the ends of the strips of litmus-paper. If they have become reddened, wet the blocks with the alkaline solution (p. 45), until they have increased 30% in weight and use them as wet gun-cotton.

If the moistened litmus strips have not become reddened after one hour's exposure, replace the blocks in the jar, close it tight and replace it in its box.

Monthly Inspection.—Even if no change is observed in the litmus-paper at the weekly inspections the test just described, with freshly moistened blue litmus-paper strips, is to be applied to all dry gun-cotton once each month and this constitutes the *monthly inspection*. If the test shows the gun-cotton to be acid, the gun-cotton should be wet with the alkaline solution (p. 45), until it has increased 30% in weight, and then used as wet gun-cotton.

INSPECTION OF WET GUN-COTTON.

Quartely Inspection.—The wet gun-cotton is packed in the Service and Exercise cases and contains from 30% to 35% of water. The gross weight of gun-cotton and case is marked upon each case. These cases are to be separately weighed every three months and any loss in the gross weight made up by the addition of pure water poured through the filling-hole, which should then be carefully closed.

PRECAUTIONS TO BE TAKEN IN INSPECTION.

Do not handle the gun-cotton with the bare hand. Never touch litmus-paper with the bare hand. Blue litmus-paper may become reddened by the acid substances exuded from the skin. Litmus-paper should always be handled with the forceps provided in the Chemical Box.

Always moisten the litmus-paper before making the test, using the distilled water provided in the Chemical Box. Hold the litmus-paper strip in the forceps, dip one of the glass rods, provided in the Chemical Box, in the bottle of distilled water and then apply the moist rod to the paper. The litmus-paper must be moist, only, and not reeking with water. Should the supply of water in the Chemical Box be exhausted, water distilled on board, or fresh rain water, may be used, provided it first be tested and found free from acid reaction.

Make a comparative test to prove that there is, or is not, an acid reaction. As blue litmus-paper may sometimes become slightly reddened when moistened with distilled water only, a comparison should always be made by taking two pieces of fresh blue litmus-paper and moistening one with distilled water and the other with dilute vinegar.

Always examine the test papers by white light. Litmus-paper will present a reddish appearance in any apartment that is shellacked or colored; the examination of test papers should therefore be made only in a light room or in the open air.

Do not mistake iron rust for pasty yellow spots. Gun-cotton sometimes becomes rusted in the course of manufacture, or from the cases in which it is packed. The rust does no harm.

Avoid unnecessary handling of the blocks, as they are apt to flake and crumble.

ALKALINE SOLUTION.

The alkaline solution refered to above is made by dissolving four ounces of dry carbonate of soda in one gallon of rain or distilled water. When it is found necessary to wet dry gun-cotton this solution may be poured into the jar holding the blocks.

RULES FOR DRYING GUN-COTTON.

Wet gun-cotton primers can be dried by any of the following methods:—
1. Exposure in a steam-drier.
2. " to calcium chloride. ($Ca\ Cl_2$).
3. " in a dry atmosphere.

The quantity of dry gun-cotton primers that are furnished being very small, the stock should be replenished as fast as used by drying the wet blocks removed from the torpedoes in priming them.

DRYING BY EXPOSURE IN A STEAM-DRIER.

The steam-drier must be located above the water-line, remote from fires and lamps and where it will not be subject to disarrangement. Its supply of steam is to be derived from a suitable part of the steam-heating appartus of the ship or from any other convenient source of low-pressure steam by piping fitted at the Navy Yard.

The blocks to be dried are separately weighed, the weight of each marked on it with a soft lead-pencil (never putting labels of any kind on the gun-cotton) and then strung on the rods, with the iron washers strung between adjacent blocks, and placed in the baskets of the drier. The baskets are put in the drier, the door is closed, the thermometer put in place, steam is turned on and the ventilating openings are adjusted.

The baskets, rods and washers must be kept free from dirt and oil.

The temperature of the drying chamber must not exceed 100° F.

After each day's heating carefully remove and weigh each block, re-mark it and proceed with the drying.

This process should be continued until the blocks no longer lose weight, when all but a small percentage of moisture will have been expelled. It has been found by experiment, however, that gun-cotton containing as much as 13% of water can be relied on to detonate, the service fulminate of mercury detonator being used.

When the drying is complete remove the blocks from the drier, place them, while still warm, in the glass jars, with strips of blue litmus-paper between them and close the jars tight. They will then be stowed and inspected as dry gun-cotton.

If the process of drying is not continuous the blocks must be kept in a powder tank, closed tight, when the drier is not in operation.

DRYING BY EXPOSURE TO CALCIUM CHLORIDE ($CaCl_2$).

This method requires: — 5 lbs. calcium chloride ($CaCl_2$), 1 empty powder tank and 3 baking pans.

The calcium chloride ($CaCl_2$) is cheap and can readily be obtained from any dealer in chemicals; it must not be confounded with chloride of lime or bleaching powder (CaO_2Cl_2). The latter has a strong odor of chlorine and, if used instead of the calcium chloride ($CaCl_2$), might cause decomposition of gun-cotton. The former is odorless and has no bleaching properties. To distinguish whether the substance has any bleaching properties, stir a small portion in an equal volume of water and immerse a piece of blue litmus-paper in the mixture. If the color disappears from the paper when dry (turning white), the substance is chloride of lime or bleaching powder (CaO_2Cl_2) and must not be used.

The powder tank can be readily procured on board ship; care must be taken that it closes easily and air-tight.

The baking pans should be of such a size that three of them will cover the bottom of the tank when placed alongside of each other; made of stout tin, free from solder, and 5 to 6 inches deep.

Divide the calcium chloride between the three pans and place these pans, which must be clean and free from oil or grease, in the oven of the galley and allow them to remain there until all traces of moisture disappears. Stir the calcium chloride occasionally with a clean metal rod to expose the lower particles. Break it into pieces the size of a pigeon's egg. When all traces of moisture have disappeared remove the pans to a dry place and allow them to cool. The calcium chloride must not be put in the tank, nor the gun-cotton exposed to it, while warm. Place the tank in some suitable location where it will not be disturbed and, when the calcium chloride is cooled, place the pans in the bottom of the tank and lay over them a copper sieve, tinned copper wire being the best. Then place the blocks to be dried on the sieve and close the tank. Open the tank every 3 or 4 days, weigh the blocks, marking the weight and date with a soft lead-pencil on them and dry the calcium chloride as before. Continue this until the blocks have ceased to lose weight. While the calcium chloride is drying, the blocks are to be kept in the tank, which must be closed to exclude the moisture in the air. When they have ceased to lose weight stow them in the glass jars for dry gun-cotton primers, taking care to lay between them strips of blue litmus-paper, and treat them according to the rules laid down for dry gun-cotton.

This opperation is independent of the condition of the atmosphere and only requires the care mentioned.

DRYING BY EXPOSURE IN A DRY ATMOSPHERE.

String the blocks to be dried on a wood, brass or copper rod or pipe, which must be free from dirt and oil, or place them on a shelf made of wire netting, separating the blocks from each other to expose all surfaces freely to the air; suspend the rod or shelf in some suitable place not in the vicinity of the galley or other fires, where the blocks will be freely exposed to the air, and be under cover.

Expose the blocks only when the atmosphere is dry;

at all other times keep them in an empty powder tank, in the immediate vicinity of the place selected for drying, kept closed to exclude moisture. Weigh the blocks every two days, noting the date and weight with a soft lead-pencil on them. Continue the drying until the blocks show no loss of weight for two consecutive weighings; then place them in the glass jars, with strips of blue litmus-paper between, and treat them acccording to the rules given for dry gun-cotton primers.

This plan can only be carried out in dry climates.

Avoid unnecessary handling of the blocks, as they are apt to flake and crumble.

MISCELLANEOUS DATA.

Dimensions of gun-cotton blocks
    length........ 2.9 inches.
    width .... 2.9 "
    height .... $\begin{cases} 2.0 " \text{ for full sized blocks.} \\ 0.5 " \text{ for primer blocks.} \end{cases}$

Diameter of detonator hole $= \frac{7}{16}$ inch.

Pressure applied to blocks in the final press $= 6800$ lbs. per square inch.

Average gravimetric density of compressed dry gun-cotton $= 1.287$.

Average weight of one cubic inch of compressed dry gun-cotton $= 325$ grains, $= 0.743$ oz.

Weight of water added to each pound of dry gun-cotton when issued to the service as wet gun-cotton (approximately 35%) $= 0.35$ lb. $= 5.6$ oz.

APPENDIX.

DUTIES OF THE INSPECTOR OF ORDNANCE.—LIST OF ARTICLES IN OUTFIT, WEIGHTS AND STOWAGE SPACE.

DUTIES OF THE INSPECTOR OF ORDNANCE AT THE NAVY YARD IN CONNECTION WITH THE TORPEDO OUTFIT OF A SHIP.

GUN-COTTON MAGAZINE.

He will carefully inspect the gun-cotton magazine, satisfy himself that it is constructed in accordance with the Ordnance Instructions concerning shell-rooms, and the directions given on pages 40 and 41 Spar-Torpedo Instructions, that it is of sufficient size to stow the portion of the torpedo outfit defined in the "Table showing Weight, Space and Place of Stowage of Articles in Spar-Torpedo Outfit" and will prepare a plan of stowage.

TORPEDO STORE-ROOM.

He will carefully inspect the torpedo store-room, satisfy himself that it is in a proper position with regard to battery and boilers, that it is not exposed to undue changes of temperature, or to accidental admission of water, and that it is of sufficient capacity and conveniently arranged to stow the portion of the outfit defined in "Table showing Weight, Space and Place of Stowage of Articles in Spar-Torpedo Outfit."

BATTERY LOCKER.

He will carefully inspect the battery locker and see that it is in a proper position with regard to the great-gun battery and the boilers. It should, preferably, be in a good light.

SHIP'S SPARS AND FITTINGS.

He will, while the ship's spars and fittings are being made and when they are in place, inspect them carefully, satisfy himself that the spar-bands are properly spaced and in line to receive the secondary spar and report to the Bureau the position and class of the heel-fittings and the leads of topping-lifts and guys, with his opinion of their efficiency and convenience.

PERMANENT WIRES.

He will ascertain what firing-apparatus the Bureau intends to place on board and make a requisition for the necessary wire and terminals.

Upon the receipt of these articles he will locate the firing-apparatus and prepare and place the permanent wires and terminals.

He will cause a plan showing the lead of the different wires to be made, and will send copies to the Bureau and to the Torpedo Station, and will furnish one to the commanding officer of the vessel.

No fixed rules can be given for leading permanent wires. The general method of leading the upper-deck wires, manner of securing to terminals and precautions to be observed, are given on pages 14 and 15. Permanent wires should also be led from the battery to the firing-point on the bridge or elsewhere. In case of electrical gun-circuits being desired, special directions or plans will be issued by the Bureau of Ordnance.

LIST OF ARTICLES IN SPAR-TORPEDO OUTFIT SUPPLIED FROM THE TORPEDO STATION.

The Spar-Torpedo Outfit for ships having one torpedo boat comprises the articles given in the list. Ships having two or more torpedo boats will have the articles in the Boat's Outfit, necessary to the simultaneous use of all the boats, increased proportionally.

Boat's Outfit.	Ship's and Boat's Outfit.	
		BOX 1.
	1	Farmer's D. E. machine, Pattern A, containing:—
	1	Firing-key.
	2	Machine connecting wires (12 feet long).
	1	Crank.
		BOX 2.
1	1	Reel box, containing:—
300	300	Feet double-conductor insulated cable.
1	1	Crank.
		BOX 3.
1	1	Supply box, containing:—
1	1	Monkey wrench.
3	3	Open end wrenches. — One end fits the screw-cover of the torpedo case; the other, the screw-bolts that secure the spindle.
1	1	Rectifier, — a wooden rod, marked in inches, for lining the blocks in the primer case.
6	12	Pieces of emery cloth, — for brightening wires and removing rust.
1	2	Pairs of cutting plyers, — for general use in cutting and working wires.
1	2	Pieces of okonite tape, — for insulating naked wires when not exposed to water.
2	2	Earth-plates, — copper plates (coated with tin to prevent rust).
12	24	Pieces of rubber tubing, — for insulating splices.
1	1	Sample splice, — for instruction.
1	2	Spools of hemp twine, — for securing rubber tubing.
1	2	Knives, — for cleaning wires and for general use.
1	1	Screw driver, — for general use.

Boat's Outfit.	Ship's and Boat's Outfit.	BOX 3. (*Continued.*)
6	12	Dummy detonators (painted white), — for instruction.
1	1	Sample detonator splice, — for instruction.
1	1	Dummy gunpowder fuze, — for instruction.
24	36	Spherical rubber packings.
36	36	Paper fasteners.
2	2	Safety pins for circuit-closer (spare).
1	1	Spring for circuit-closer (spare).
1	1	⅜ by 16 screw-tap, — to cut a thread for spar screws.
12	12	Screws for boat's steel spars, — to secure the two parts of a boat spar.
4	4	Reeving-lines, — for reeving leading-wires through the boat's spars.
2	2	Reeving-line weights, — to reeve the reeving-lines through the boat's spars.

BOX 4.

	1	Wire box, ship's, containing:—
	4	Spar leading-wires.
	2	Machine connecting wires (12 feet long, spare).

BOX 5.

	4	Spar-bands with key-ways.
	4	" (ordinary).
	24	Wood screws.

BOX 6.

4	8	Tin boxes, containing:—
4	8	Detonator-blocks.
32	64	Detonators.

BOX 7.

32	32	Gunpowder igniters.
18	18	" fuzes.

BOX 8.

2	4	Glass jars with corks, containing:—
12	24	Blocks dry gun-cotton.

BOX 9.

	1	Testing and firing plate (when specially ordered).

BOXES 10 AND 11.

	12	Secondary spars, ship's.
	12	Keys for same.

BOXES 12 AND 13.

12	12	Secondary spars, boat's.
12	12	Toggles for same.

BOX 14.

1	1	Farmer's D. E. machine, Pattern C, containing:—
2	2	Machine connecting wires (12 feet long).
1	1	Crank.

Boat's Outfit.	Ship's and Boat's Outfit.	BOX 15.
1	1	Wire box, boat's, containing:—
4	4	Spar leading-wires.
2	2	Machine connecting wires (12 feet long, spare).
4	4	Secondary spar caps.
4	4	Rivets for same.
4	4	Secondary spar butts.
4	4	Rivets for same.
		BOX 16.
1	1	Chemical box, containing:—
2	2	Pair forceps.
2	2	" scissors.
2	2	Bottles distilled water.
2	2	" for litmus-paper.
½	½	Quire litmus-paper.
1	1	Tin cylinder for same.
2	2	Pounds carbonate of soda (dry).
1	1	Piece boiled tape.
2	2	Glass rods.
		BOX 17.
2	2	Spar clamps.
1	1	Set of boat fittings, Pattern B, as follows:—
2	2	Heel-rests.
2	2	Hinge-plates.
2	2	⅝ bolts with nuts,—for securing heel-rests to hinge-plates.
2	2	Swivel crutches,—each with a hinged top and two rollers, secured together by studs, rivets and pins.
2	2	Bearings secured to crutches with bolts and washers.
1	1	Cross-beam with two bearings riveted on.
2	2	Hoods, (right and left),—each fitted with two bolts for securing to the cross-beam.
2	2	Securing rods,—for securing elevating-arms to cross-beam.
2	2	Elevating-arms with cog-wheels attached.
2	2	Plate washers,—for holding elevating-arms on cross-beams.
2	2	Nuts on ends of securing rods,—to hold washers in place.
2	2	Guide rings,—each fitted with a roller secured by studs and split pins.
2	2	Screw-nuts,—each fitted with a lock-screw, to secure guide rings to elevating-arms.
2	2	Worm shafts,—each in two parts, joined by a hook-coupling.
2	2	Elevating-wheels,—with pins for securing same to worm-shafts.
2	2	Clutches, consisting of the following parts:—
2	2	Bearings.

Boat's Outfit.	Ship's and Boat's Outfit.	BOX 17. (*Continued.*)
2	2	Sleeves,—with trunnions and lugs.
2	2	Yoke-links.
2	2	Detaching-levers,—each with transverse roller attached.
2	2	Pins,—for locking detaching-levers.
4	4	Bolts with split pins,—for securing parts of clutch together.
16	16	⅝ bolts,—for securing hinge-plates, swivel-crutch bearings and clutch-bearings to boat.*
16	16	⅝ phosphor-bronze nuts for same.
4	4	¾ bolts,—for securing cross-beam bearings to deck.*
4	4	¾ phosphor-bronze nuts for same.

*Note.— These bolts are supplied at the Navy Yard where the boats are fitted.

BOX 18.

1	1	Testing magneto.

BOXES 19 TO 22. (*Both inclusive*).

2	2	Boat spars.
2	2	Canvas bags for same.

BOXES 23 TO 46. (*Both inclusive*).

12	24	Service Torpedoes, Pattern D.

BOXES 47 AND 48.

BOXES 49 AND 50.

12	12	Exercise Torpedoes, Pattern D, (two of which are empty).

BOXES 51 AND 52.

BOX 53.

12	24	Service Torpedo spindles.
12	12	Exercise " "
24	36	Torpedo pins.
4	8	" " (spare).

BOX 54.

	1	Ship's firing-battery.
	1	Battery tester (6.5 ohms).
1	1	Boat's firing-battery.
2	2	Spare cells for same.
1	1	Battery tester (4 ohms).
1	2	Hand-firing keys.
3	5	Pounds sal-ammoniac.
12	12	Spare fuze-bridges,—for testing batteries.

Boat's Outfit.	Ship's and Boat's Outfit.	BOX 55.
1	1	Steam drier.

BOX 56.

4	4	Circuit-closers, — for Contact Torpedo.
4	4	Spherical rubber packings for same.
4	4	Rubber diaphragms for same.
16	16	Brass screws, — for attaching circuit-closer.

BOX 57.

1	1	Contact spar leading-wires.
2	2	Rubber diaphragms (spare).
12	12	" washers, — for Exercise Torpedo (spare).
12	24	" " — for Service Torpedo (spare).
4	8	Spherical rubber packings (spare).
		In addition to the above, if no testing and firing-plate is furnished,
	2	Electric switches.

Two Copies of the Torpedo Instructions, corrected to date of issue, will be furnished to each vessel receiving a torpedo outfit.

These copies will be sent by mail, simultaneously with the issue of the outfit, addressed to the Inspector of Ordnance at the Navy Yard at which the vessel is fitted out.

This book is corrected to

Terminals and insulated wire for permanent wires will be furnished as required.

The Bureau of Ordnance will designate which of the following will be supplied :—

2	Electric switches.
1	Testing and firing-plate.

SUPPLIED FROM NAVY YARD.

		Torpedo spars for ship.
		Fittings for same.
16	16	⅝ bolts, — for securing boat-fittings to boat.
4	4	¾ " " " " " " "

Note. — Boxes 6, 7, 8, 23 to 46 inclusive, 49 and 50, contain explosives, which must be stowed as directed in the Instructions.

Boxes 8 and 16 contain glass and are to be handled with care.

Boxes 2, 4, 15 and 57 contain insulated wire and must be stowed in a cool place to guard against deterioration of the insulation.

All other boxes must be stowed in a dry place and the contents kept free from rust.

TABLE SHOWING WEIGHT, SPACE AND PLACE OF STOWAGE OF ARTICLES IN TORPEDO OUTFIT.

WHERE STOWED.	Invoice number of boxes.	OUTSIDE DIMENSIONS OF BOX IN INCHES			Approximate cubical space of each box.	Approximate gross weight of each box.	BOAT'S OUTFIT.			SHIP'S AND BOAT'S OUTFIT.		
		L.	W.	D.			Number of boxes.	Total approximate cubical space.	Aggregate weight.	Number of boxes.	Total approximate cubical space.	Aggregate weight.
					Cu. ft.	Lbs.		Cu. ft.	Lbs.		Cu. ft.	Lbs.
GUN-COTTON MAGAZINE.	23 to 46	11.8	11.8	17.8	1.4	72.	12	16.8	864.	24	33.6	1728.
	49, 50	13.8	12.9	17.	1.8	66.	2	3.6	132.	2	3.6	132.
	1	16.	13.5	20.5	2.6	146.	....	....	....	1	2.6	146.
	2	18.5	15.2	17.5	2.8	92.	1	2.8	92.	1	2.8	92.
	3	20.	16.	10.5	1.9	48.	1	1.9	48.	1	1.9	48.
	4	16.5	16.5	16.	2.5	67.	....	....	....	1	2.5	67.
	10, 11	98.5	14.	5.	4.	222.	....	....	....	2	8.	444.
	12, 13	102.	21.	6.	7.4	230.	2	14.8	460.	2	14.8	460.
	14	12.6	11.	10.5	1.3	54.	1	1.3	54.	1	1.3	54.
TORPEDO	15	16.6	16.6	16.	2.6	68.	1	2.6	68.	1	2.6	68.
STOREROOM.	16	19.	11.6	12.6	1.6	30.	1	1.6	30.	1	1.6	30.
	17	86.5	15.3	18.	13.8	400.	1	13.8	400.	1	13.8	400.
	18	7.8	5.3	7.5	.2	9.	1	.2	9.	1	.2	9.
	19 to 22 {	219.	8.5	6.5	7.	205.	2	14.	410.	2	14.	410.
		183.	8.5	6.5	5.8	170.	2	11.6	340.	2	11.6	340.
	53	19.8	11.6	15.1	2.	105.	1	2.	105.	2	4.	172.
	55											
	56	24.6	13.	8.2	1.5	43.	1	1.5	43.	1	1.5	43.
	57	19.5	18.5	6.6	1.3	28.5	1	1.3	28.5	1	1.3	28.5
BATTERY LOCKER.	54	15.	10.5	11.5	1.	37.5	1	1.	36.5	1	1.9	70.5
IN PLACE ON SPARS.	5	21.	16.5	7.5	1.5	80.	....	....	....	1	1.5	80.
" " DECK.	9	52.	18.5	18.5	10.4	155.	....	....	....	1	10.4	155.
SEE REGULATIONS	6	9.8	9.7	6.8	.4	10.	1	.4	10.	1	.7	20.
FOR SAME.	7	12.2	10.2	5.2	.4	11.	1	.4	11.	1	.4	11.
	8	8.2	14.2	17.5	1.2	25.	1	1.2	25.	1	2.2	49.

INDEX.

	PAGE.
After guy — ship's torpedo spar	16
Alkaline solution	45
Amount of water in wet gun-cotton	44
Apparatus for drying gun-cotton	13, 47, 48, 49
Articles for testing gun-cotton. (See Chemical box).	
" list of in outfit	52
" of torpedo outfit supplied at Navy Yard	15, 56
" " " " " from Torpedo Station	14, 52
" spare	1, 14
Bands, spar	8, 53
Batteries, firing. (See Firing-batteries).	
Battery-cell, discription	27
" cells, spare	27, 55
" locker	51
" tester	28, 55
Blocks, detonator	11, 53
" primer, dry	12, 39, 40, 41, 49, 53
Boat, firing-batteries. (See Firing-batteries).	
" fittings, Pattern B	8, 9, 10, 54, 55
" spar. (See Spar).	
" to test the circuit from	21
" wire-box	7, 54
Bow-fittings	8, 54
Box, chemical	13, 54
" gunpowder fuzes and igniters	12, 53
" reel	6, 52
" stuffing	3
" supply	8, 52
" torpedo packing	39
" wire, boats	7, 54
" " ships	6, 7, 53
Butts, secondary spar	5, 54
Cable, insulated. (See Reel box).	
Caps, secondary spar	5, 54
" " " rivets for	54
" water. (See Stuffing-boxes).	
Care and management of firing-batteries	29
" of gun-cotton and detonators	41
Case, primer. (See Primer case).	
Cell, battery	27

	PAGE.
Cells, battery, spare	27, 55
Charge, detonator	10, 42
" primer, dry. (See Primer charge).	
Calcium, chloride. (See Chloride of calcium).	
Chemical box	13, 54
Chloride of calcium	47
" " " how distinguished from chloride of lime	47
" " " test of, for bleaching properties	47
" " " to be used instead of chloride of lime	47
" " lime. (See Chloride of calcium).	
Circuit-closer, Pattern B, description	4
" " " " how attached	4, 22
" " " " " test	22, 23
" " " " necessary to be water-tight	23
" " " " number issued	4, 56
" " " " safety-pin to be in before priming	23
" " " " to be tested before priming	23
" " safety-pins, spare	53
" " spring, spare	53
" " weight of	5
Circuit testing, from ships	20
" to test the, from boats	21
Clamps, spar	10, 54
Cloth, emery	52
Commanding officer of vessel to be furnished with plan of wires	52
Condition of firing-batteries, how to test	28, 29
Connection to terminal, machine, or battery not to be made until	20, 21
Contact, fire on, when using circuit-closer, Pattern B	24
" spar leading-wires, Pattern B. (See Wires).	
" torpedo. (See Torpedo).	
Continuity of wires, testing	32, 38
Crutch, swivel	8, 54
Cutting plyers	52
Depth. (See Immersion).	
Detonator	10, 41, 42, 53
" blocks	10, 53
" bridge, resistance of	11
" care of	41
" charge	11, 42
" dummy	12, 53
" packing and stowage	10, 42
" splice sample	53
" splicing on	18
" testing, manner of	17
" when tested, to be put in safe place	17
Diaphragms, rubber	56
Distance, proper, for contact torpedo before firing	21
" " " exercise " " "	22
" " " service " " "	21

	PAGE.
Drier, steam	13, 46, 56
Dry primers. (See Primer).	
Drying apparatus, gun-cotton	13, 47, 48, 49
" gun-cotton, rules for	45
Dummy detonators	12, 53
" gun-powder fuze	53
Dynamo-electric machine, pattern A	32, 52
" " " " C	36, 53
Earth-plates	52
Electric switches	15, 56
" " and permanent wires, use of	25
" " not issued with permanent firing apparatus	15
" " " to be used as firing-keys	26
Emery cloth	52
Exercise torpedo. (See Torpedo).	
Fasteners, paper	53
Fire at will, contact torpedoes	24
" on contact, contact torpedoes	24
" torpedoes using A machine and firing-key	21
" " " C "	21
" " " battery and hand-firing key	21
Firing-batteries	27
" " boats	28, 55
" " how to test condition of	28, 30
" " management and care of	29
" " no connection to be made with until	20, 21
" " not to be used to test the circuit	21
" " number furnished	27
" " ships	28, 55
Firing-key, D. E. machine, pattern A	34, 52
" " " " " " to test	36
Fittings, boats. (See Boat fittings).	
" bow	8
" heel, ship's torpedo spar	16
" " " " " substitute for	16
" ship's spar	16, 56
Forward guy, ship's torpedo spar, how fitted	16
Fuze bridges, spare	55
" gunpowder, dummy	53
" " splicing on	25
Fuzes, gunpowder	12, 53
Fuzing torpedoes. (See Torpedo).	
Glass jars for dry primers	12, 41, 53
Gun-cotton, amount in torpedo outfit	40
" " " of water in when wet	44
" " apparatus for drying	13, 57, 48, 49
" " articles for testing. (See Chemical box).	
" " care of	41
" " dry, packing and stowage of	39

	PAGE.
Gun-cotton, inspection of	42
" " " " precautions to be taken	44
" " magazine	41
" " miscellaneous data	49
" " primers. (See Primers).	
" " rules for drying	45
" " test of. (See Inspection of gun-cotton).	
" " removed in priming, where placed	17, 22
" " wet, packing and stowage of	39
Gunpowder fuze, dummy	53
" " splicing on	25
" fuzes	12, 53
" igniters	11, 53
" torpedoes, improvised	24
Guy, after, ship's torpedo spar	16
" forward, " " " how fitted	16
Hand-firing key	31, 55
Heel fittings, ship's torpedo spar, description	16
" " " " " substitute for	16
Hemp twine	52
Horizontal distance. (See Distance).	
Igniters, gunpowder	12, 53
Immersion, proper for the exercise torpedo	22
" " " " service torpedo	21
" " " " contact torpedo	21
Improvised torpedoes, gunpowder	24
Inspection of gun-cotton	42
" " " precautions to be taken	44
Inspectors of ordnance at Navy Yard, duties of	51
Instructions, Torpedo, copies of	56
Insulated cable. (See Reel box).	
Insulating splices	38
Insulation of wires	37
" " " not to be damaged	37
" " " testing the	32
Jars, glass, for dry primers	12, 41, 53
Key for ship's secondary spar	5, 53
" hand-firing	31, 55
Knives	3
Lead-covered wires	14
Leading-wires. (See Wires).	
Lift, topping, ship's torpedo spar, how fitted	16
Lines, reeving	20, 53
" " weights	20, 53
Locker, battery	51
Machine connecting wires	6, 7, 52, 53, 54
" dynamo-electric, pattern A	32, 52
" " " " C	36, 53
" no connection to be made with until torpedo is immersed.	20, 21

	PAGE.
Magazine, gun-cotton	41
Magneto, testing	31, 32, 55
Management and care of firing-batteries	29
Monkey-wrench	52
Navy Yard, articles of torpedo outfit supplied at	14, 56
" " Inspectors of ordnance at, duties of	51
No connection to be made to terminal, battery, or machine until	20, 21
Officer commanding vessel to be furnished with plan of wires	52
Okonite tape	18, 52
Open-end wrench	52
Outfit, spar-torpedo, amount of gun-cotton in	40
" " articles of, invoice number of boxes containing.	57
" " " " list of	52
" " " " place of stowage	57
" " " " spaced occupied when boxed	57
" " " " supplied at Navy Yards	14, 56
" " " " " from Torpedo Station	48
" " " " weight of when boxed	57
" " how designated	1
" " includes	1
Packing, spherical rubber	3, 53, 56
Paper fasteners	53
Permanent wires	14, 56
" " plan to be furnished to	52
" " use of	25
Pins, safety, for circuit-closer, spare	53
" " " " " to be in before priming	23
" torpedo	5, 55
" " spare	55
Plate, testing and firing	53, 56
Plates, earth	52
Plyers, cutting	52
Precautions to be taken in inspection of gun-cotton	44
Preparation of contact torpedo	22
" " exercise " pattern D	22
" " service " " "	17
Primer blocks	12, 39, 40, 41, 53
" case, description of	2
" charge	40, 41
" not to remain long in exercise torpedo	22
" dry gun-cotton, care of	41
" " " " how packed and stowed	12, 39, 41
" " " " inspection of	42
" " " " number furnished	41, 42
" " " " precautions to be observed with	42, 44
" " " " testing. (See Inspection of gun-cotton).	
" wet " " how packed	39
Priming the exercise torpedo	22
" " service torpedo	17

	PAGE.
Priming, wet gun-cotton removed in, where stowed	17, 22
Rectifier	19, 52
Reel box	6, 52
Reeving lines	20, 53
" line weights	20, 53
Resistance of detonator bridge	11
Rivets for secondary spar butts	54
" " " " caps	54
Rubber diaphragms	4, 56
" packing, spherical	3, 53, 56
" tubing	38, 52
" washers	2, 56
Rules for drying gun-cotton	45
Safety-break of contact spar leading-wires	6
" " to be kept open until	24
Sample splice	52
" " detonator	53
Safety-pin circuit-closer, spare	53
" " " " to be in before priming	23
Screw driver	52
" tap	53
Screws for boat-spar, pattern A	53
Secondary spar. (See Spar).	
Service torpedo. (See Torpedo).	
Shipping contact torpedo, safety-pin to be in before	23
" secondary spar. (See Spar).	
" torpedo. (See Torpedo).	
Ship's firing-batteries. (See Firing-batteries).	
" testing circuit from	20
" torpedo spar. (See Spar).	
" wire box	6, 53
Solution, alkaline	45
Spar-bands	8, 53
" boat, pattern A	10, 55
" " " " screws for	53
" " " " to be taken apart when not in use	10
" clamps	10, 54
" leading-wires. (See Wires).	
" secondary, butts	5, 54
" " " rivets	54
" " caps	5, 54
" " " rivets	54
" " keys	5, 54
" " pattern A, description	5
" " " " difference between boats and ships	5
" " " " how packed for boats	5, 54
" " " " " " " ships	5, 54
" " " " number supplied	5
" " pattern A, shipping	19

	PAGE.
Spar secondary, pattern A, toggles	5, 53
" ship's, description	15
" " fittings	16, 56
" " number supplied	15
" torpedo. (See Torpedo).	
Spare articles	1, 14
Spherical rubber packing	56
Spindle for torpedo. (See Torpedo).	
Splice wire, insulating of	38
" " sample	52
" detonator, sample	53
" towing strain on, how to prevent	19
Splicing on detonator	18
" " gunpowder fuze	25
" wires	37
Spring for circuit-closer, spare	53
Steam-drier	13, 46, 56
Store-room, torpedo	51
Strain, towing on splices, how to prevent	19
Stuffing boxes	3
Supply-box	8, 52
Switches, electric. (See Electric switches)	
" " and permanent wires, use of	25
Swivel-crutch	8, 54
Table showing weight, space, and place of stowage of articles	57
Tape, okonite	18, 52
Terminals	15
" connection with not to be made until	20
Test circuit through circuit-closer, pattern B, how to	22, 23
" condition of firing batteries, how to	28, 30
Tester, battery	28, 55
Test, gun-cotton. (See Inspection of gun-cotton).	
Testing and firing-plate	53, 56
" circuit-closer, pattern B	22
" circuit from boat	21
" " " ship	20
" continuity of wires	32, 38
" detonator circuit in contact torpedoes	24
" " manner of	17
" " when, put in a safe place	17
" gun-cotton, articles for. (See Chemical box).	
" insulation of wires	32
" magneto	31, 32, 55
Toggles, secondary spar	5, 53
Topping lift, ship's spar	16
Torpedo, contact, circuit-closer to be tested before priming	22
" " fuzing	23
" " no connection to be made until	21
" " preparation of	22

	PAGE.
Torpedo, contact, priming	23
" " proper distance and immersion	21
" " shipping	23
" " safety-pin to be in	23
" " splicing on detonator for	23
" " testing circuit	24
" " to fire at will	24
" " " " on contact	24
" " spar leading-wires, pattern B	7, 22, 23, 24
" exercise, pattern D, description	2
" " " " fuzing	22
" " " " necessary to be closed water-tight	3, 22
" " " " no connection to be made until	20, 21
" " " " number issued	2, 40
" " " " outfit of	40, 55
" " " " packed	39
" " " " preparation of	22
" " " " primer not to remain in long	22
" " " " priming	22
" " " " shipping	22
" " " " spindle packed	5, 55
" " " " splicing detonator on	22
" " " " testing	22
" " " " weight, empty	3
" " " " " of charge	3
" " " " when issued filled with wet gun-cotton	3, 39, 44
" " proper distance and immersion	22
" Instructions, copies of	56
" outfit. (See Outfit).	
" no connection to terminal, battery, or machine to be made until	20, 21
" packing boxes	39
" pins. (See Pins).	
" service and contact, proper distance and immersion	21
" " pattern D, conversion of to contact torpedo	2, 22
" " " " description	1
" " " " firing	21
" " " " fuzing	19
" " " " necessary to be closed water tight	2
" " " " no connection to be made until	20, 21
" " " " not advisable to prime long before using	17
" " " " number issued	1, 40
" " " " outfit	40, 55
" " " " preparation of	17
" " " " primer-case	2
" " " " priming	17
" " " " shipping	19

	PAGE.
Torpedo, service, pattern D, splicing detonator on	18
" " " " spindle	2, 55
" " " " testing	20, 21
" " " " weight, empty........................	2
" " " " " of charge......................	2
" " " " when issued filled with wet gun-cotton	2, 39, 44
" spars, ship's..	15
" " " number of....................................	15
Torpedo Station, articles supplied from	52
" store-room	51
Torpedoes, firing, using A machine and firing-key.................	21
" " " C "	21
" " " battery and hand-firing key................	21
" gunpowder improvised.....................................	24
" how named..	1
" " packed and marked	39
" " to be stowed on board ship..........................	39
" intended use of...	1
" when received on board, what to do with.................	39
Towing strain on splices, how to prevent..........................	19
Tubing, rubber..	38, 52
Twine, hemp...	52
Use of permanent wires and electrical switches	25
" " leading-wires with circuit-closer, pattern B	22, 23, 24
Washers, rubber...	2, 56
Water, amount in wet gun-cotton	44
" caps. (See Stuffing Boxes).	
Weights, reeving line..	20, 53
Wet gun-cotton, amount of water in................................	44
" " " packing and stowage of	39
" " " removed in priming, where placed	17, 22
" primers. (See Primers).	
Will, to fire at, contact torpedo, using circuit-closer, pattern B	24
Wire box, boat's..	7, 54
" " ship's..	6, 7, 53
Wire, continuity of, testing the......................................	32, 38
" insulation of..	37
" " " not to be damaged.............................	37
" " " testing the	32
" splice, insulating	38
Wires, contact spar leading, pattern B.............................	7, 22, 23, 24
" lead-covered	14
" machine connecting....................................	6, 7, 52, 53, 54
" permanent. (See Permanent).	
" " plan of, to be furnished to......................	52
" spar leading, how marked..................................	7
" " " boats..................................	7
" " " " to be led through spar	20

	PAGE.
Wires, spar leading, never to be connected to terminals, battery, or machine until	20, 21
" " " ship's	6, 54
" " " " to be stopped to spar	19
" splicing	37
Wrench, monkey	52
Wrenches open-end	52

PLATES.

PLATE I.

Service Torpedo. — Pattern D.

A barrel.
B lower head.
C upper "
g, h splices between leading-wires and detonator-wires.
K handle.
l lugs for handle.
k "   " spindle.
i, i screw-holes for attaching circuit-closer.
n screw-rib for screw-cover.
r projection on handle shipping into spindle.
t screw-bolts securing spindle to lugs.
H spindle.
L spar leading-wires.
M water-cap.
P primer-case.
O screw-cover.
w rubber washer.
G spherical rubber packing.
D, D dry gun-cotton primer.
x detonator.
Y wet charge.

PLATE I.

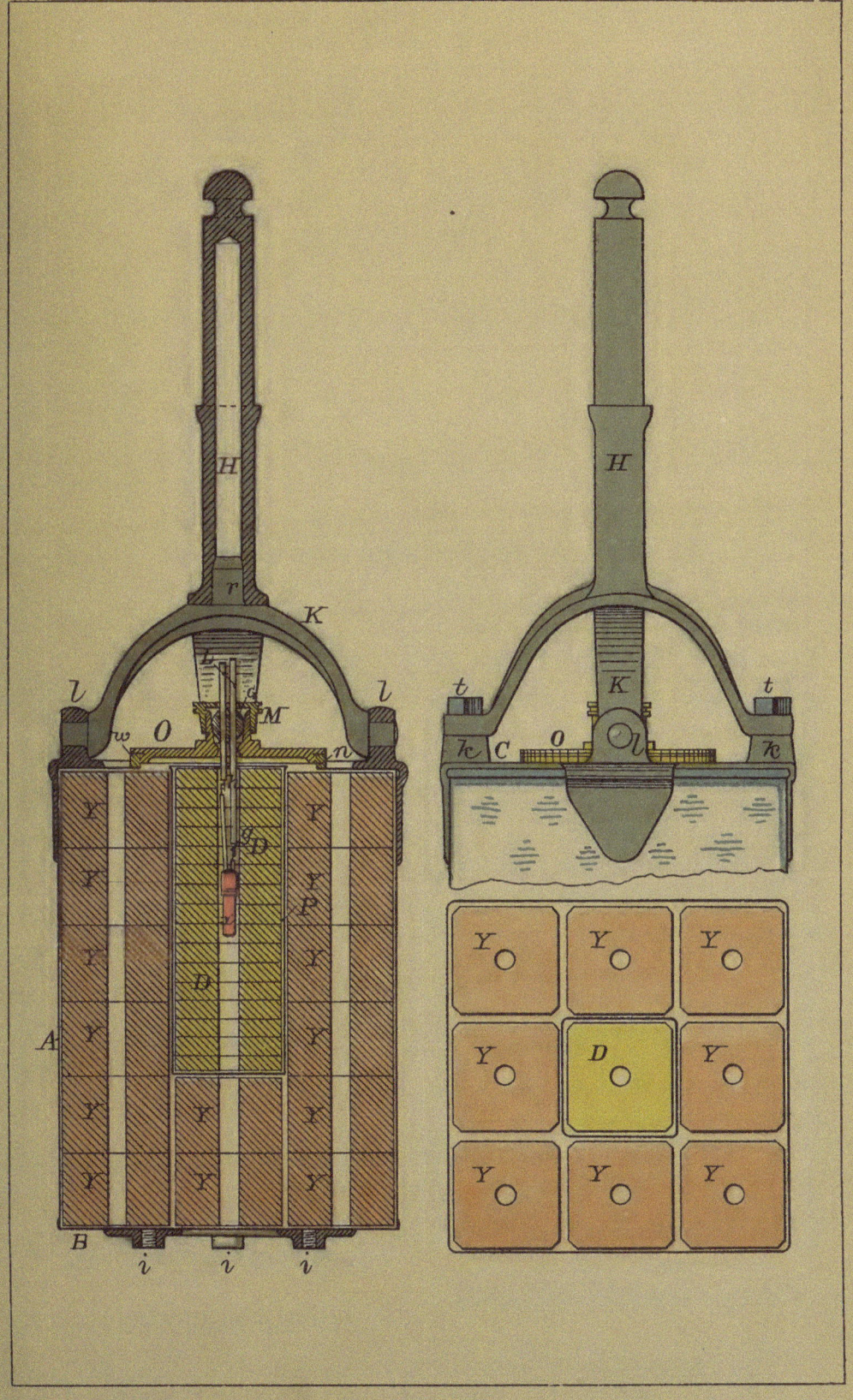

PLATE II.

Exercise Torpedo. — Pattern D.

c case.
d lower loop.
e, e loops for transportation thumb-screw and for spindle.
f throw-back hinge with thumb-screw.
H spindle.
O cover.
w rubber washer.
M water-cap.
G spherical rubber packing.
Y, Y, Y, Y wet charge.
D, D, D, D dry primer.
x detonator.
L spar leading-wires.
g, h splices between leading-wires and detonator-wires.

PLATE II.

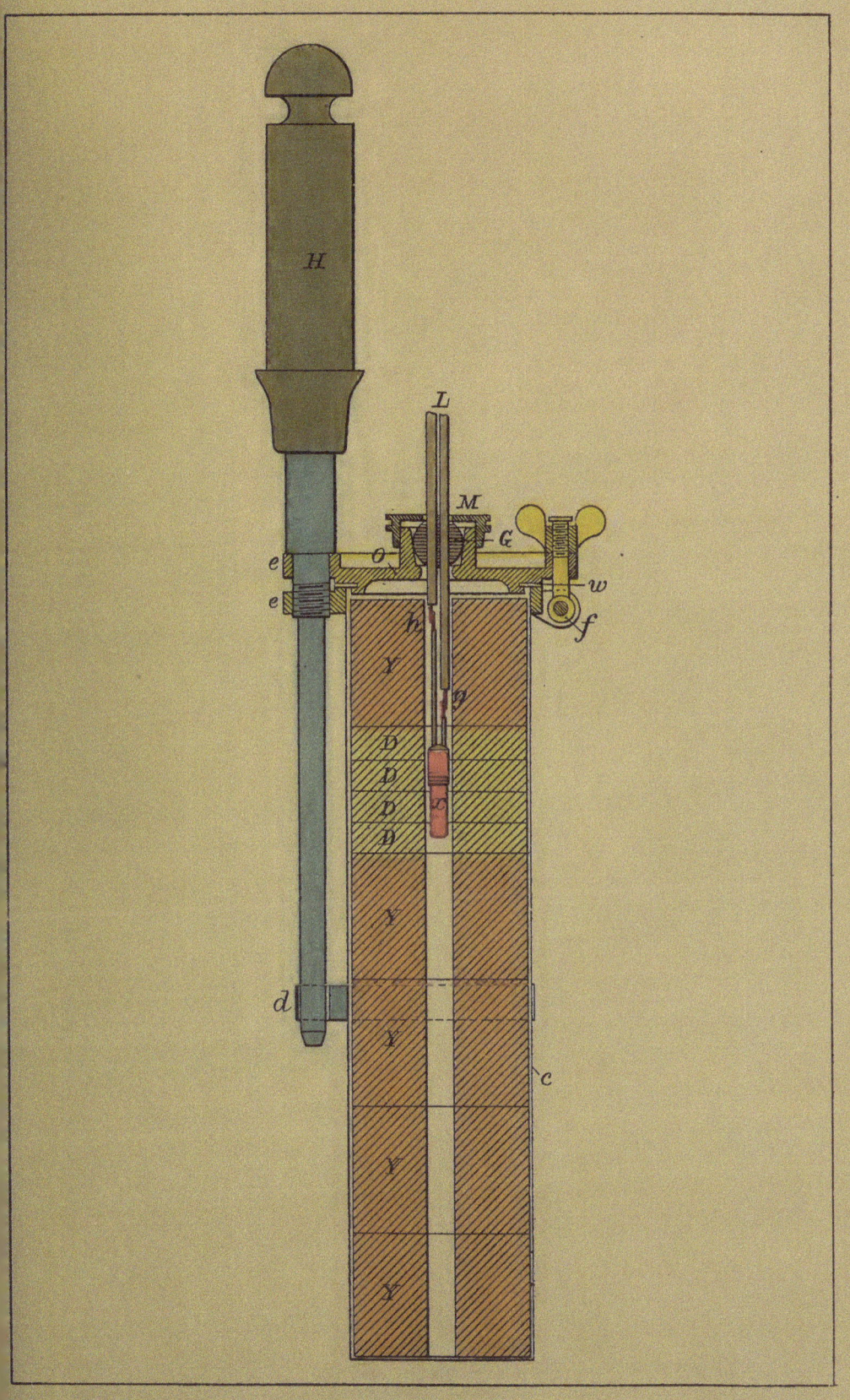

PLATE III.

Circuit-closer. — Pattern B. — Contact Torpedo.

A hollow brass casting.
M water-cap.
G spherical rubber packing.
O, O feet for attaching circuit-closer to service torpedo, Pattern D.
B inner brass plunger.
C spiral spring.
N ebonite collar.
I, I binding-posts.
E contact springs.
t screw-cover.
s, s contact arms.
K outer plunger.
l safety-pin.
V rubber diaphragm.
k friction-plate.

PLATE III.

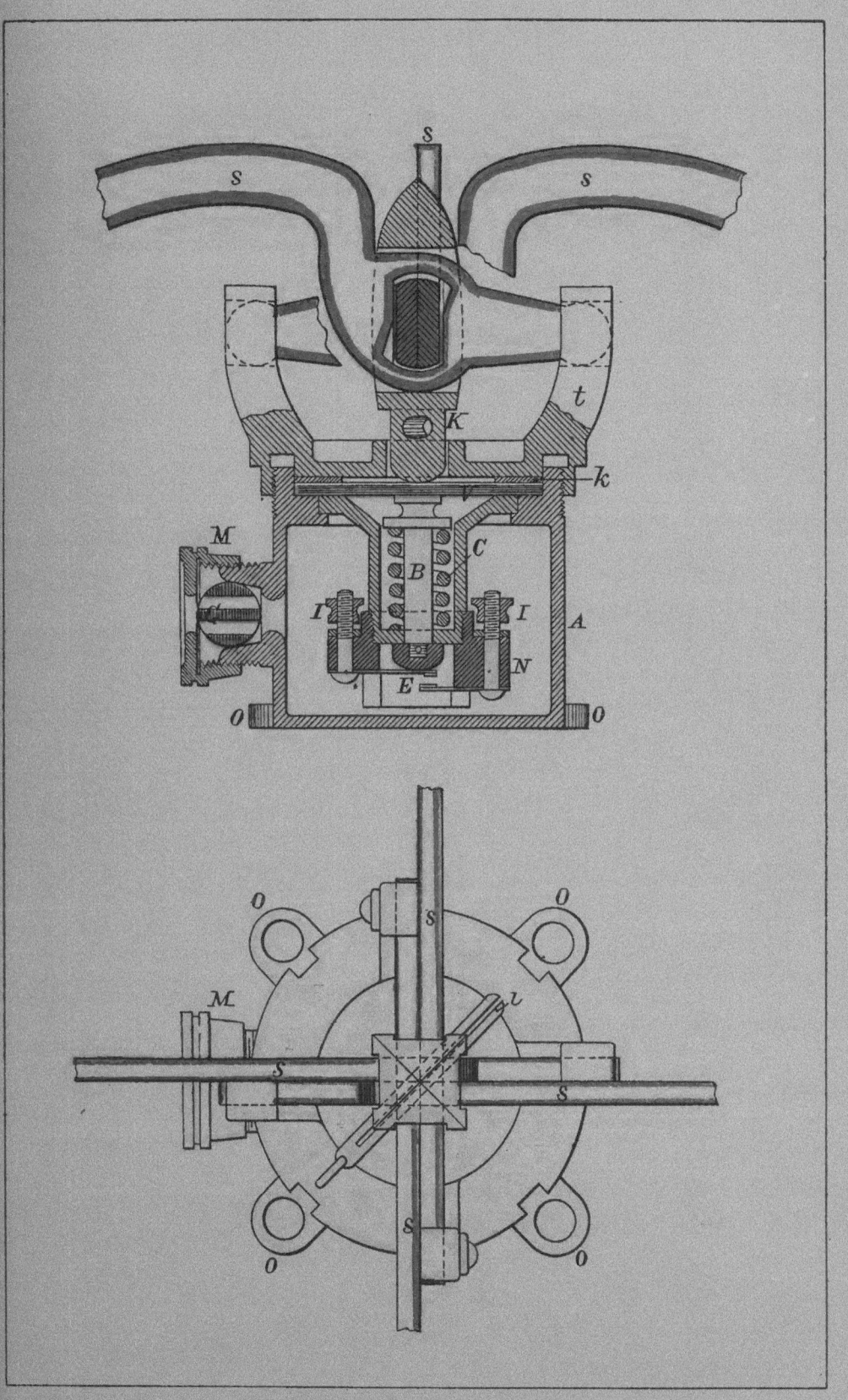

PLATE IV.

SECONDARY SPARS.

Fig. 1, Ship's. — Pattern A.

A main spar.
B secondary spar.
a, a spar-bands.
b key-way.
c key.
l hole for torpedo-pin.
m torpedo-pin.

Fig. 2, Boat's. — Pattern A.

R main spar.
H secondary spar.
i butt.
k cap.
g toggle.
l hole for torpedo-pin.
m torpedo-pin.

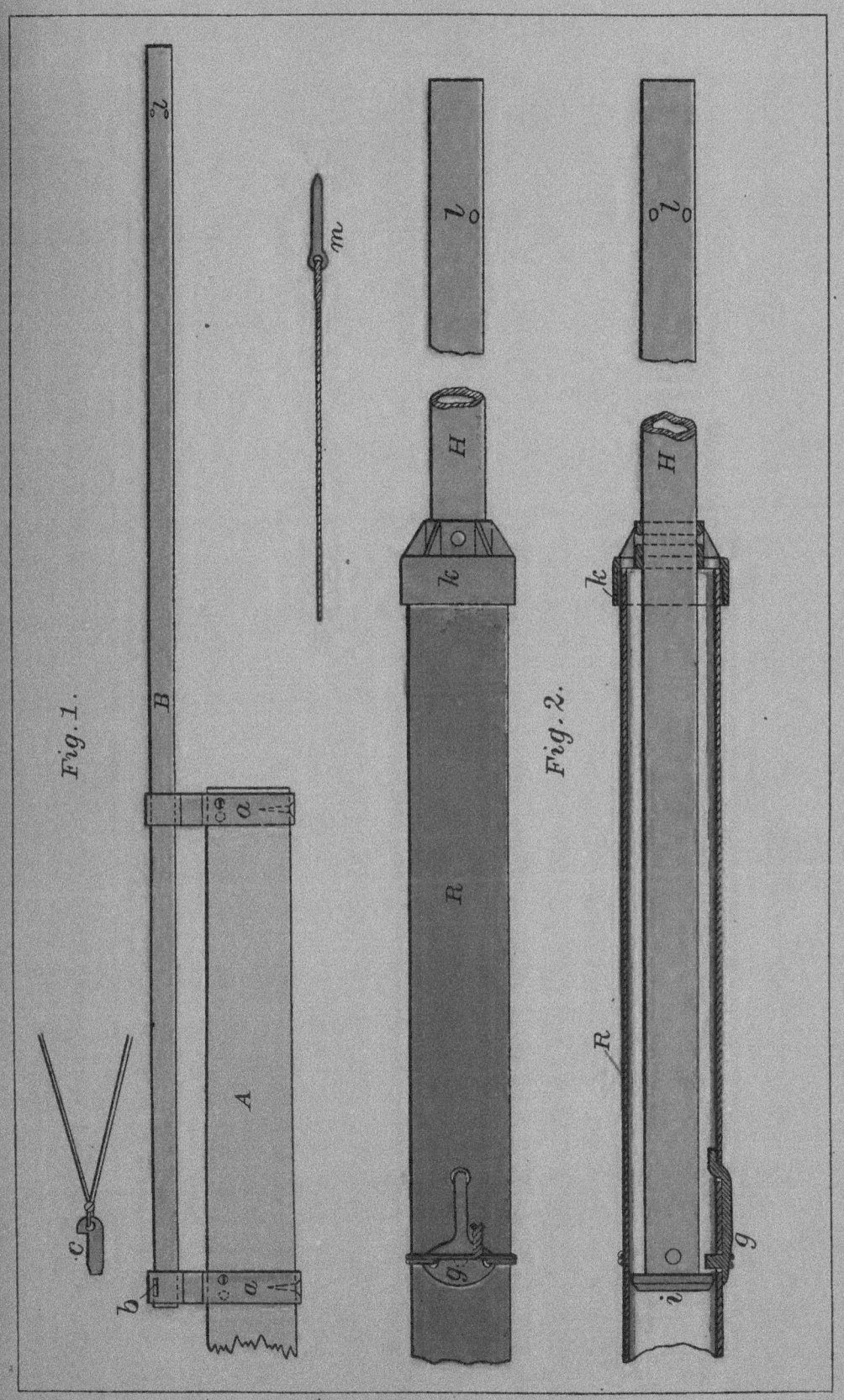

PLATE V.

Contact Spar-leading Wires.—Pattern B.

B battery.
C contact torpedo.
x circuit-closer.
D contact spar leading-wires.
H hand-firing key.
S safety-break.

PLATE V.

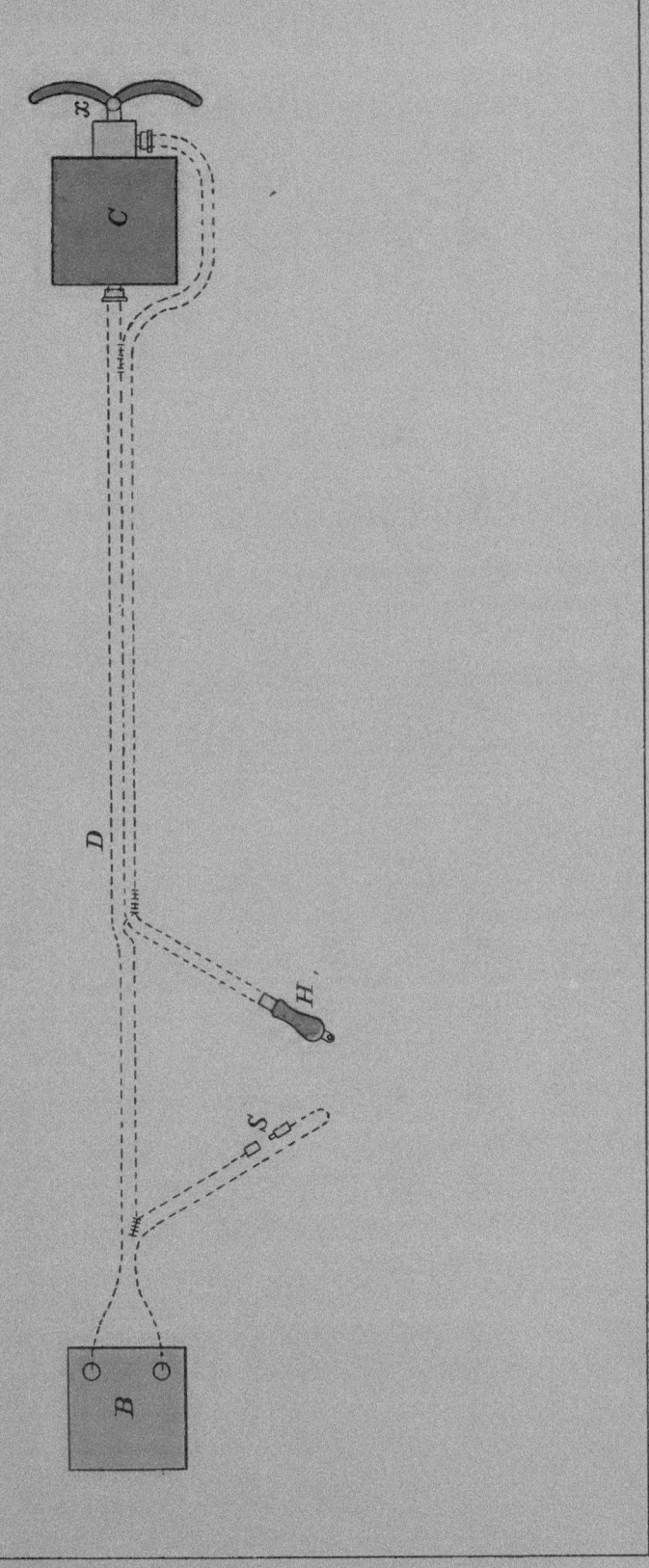

PLATE VI.

Spar-Torpedo Boat-fittings. — Pattern B.

S heel-rest.
H swivel-crutch.
R cross-beam.
D "   bearing, rivetted to cross-beam and bolted through rail.
E elevating-arm.
m plate washer.
n nut on end of securing rod.
G guide-ring.
K gear on elevating-arm.
M worm.
N worm-shaft, forward length.
O "   "   after   "
X hook-coupling.
P elevating-wheel.
Q clutch.
L detaching lever.
T torpedo.
A main spar.
B secondary spar.

PLATE VI.

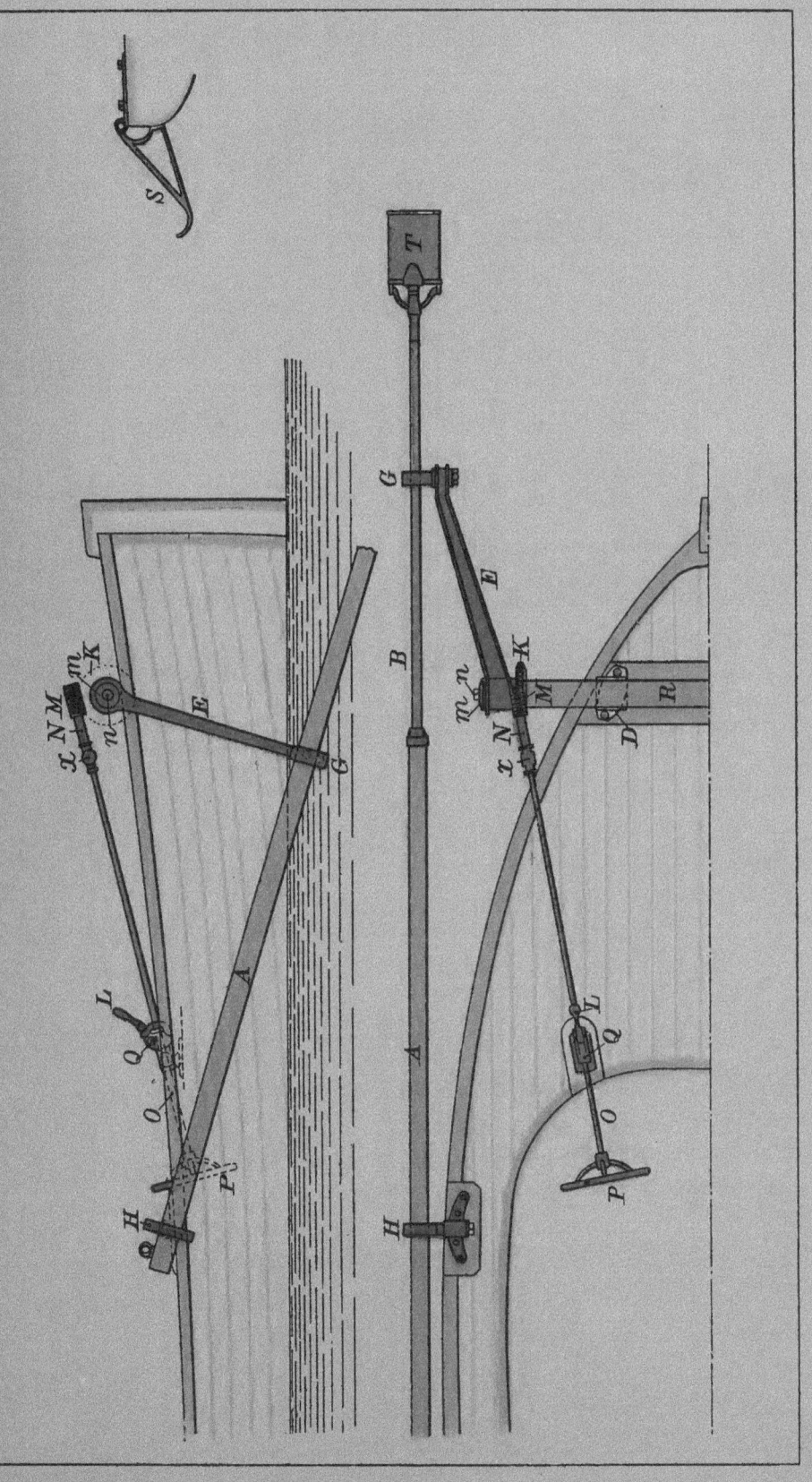

PLATE VII.

Junction of Tubes Forming Boat's Spar. — Pattern A.

A large tube.
B small tube.
c, c rings.
d shoulder.
e screw holes.
f feather.
g score.

PLATE VII.

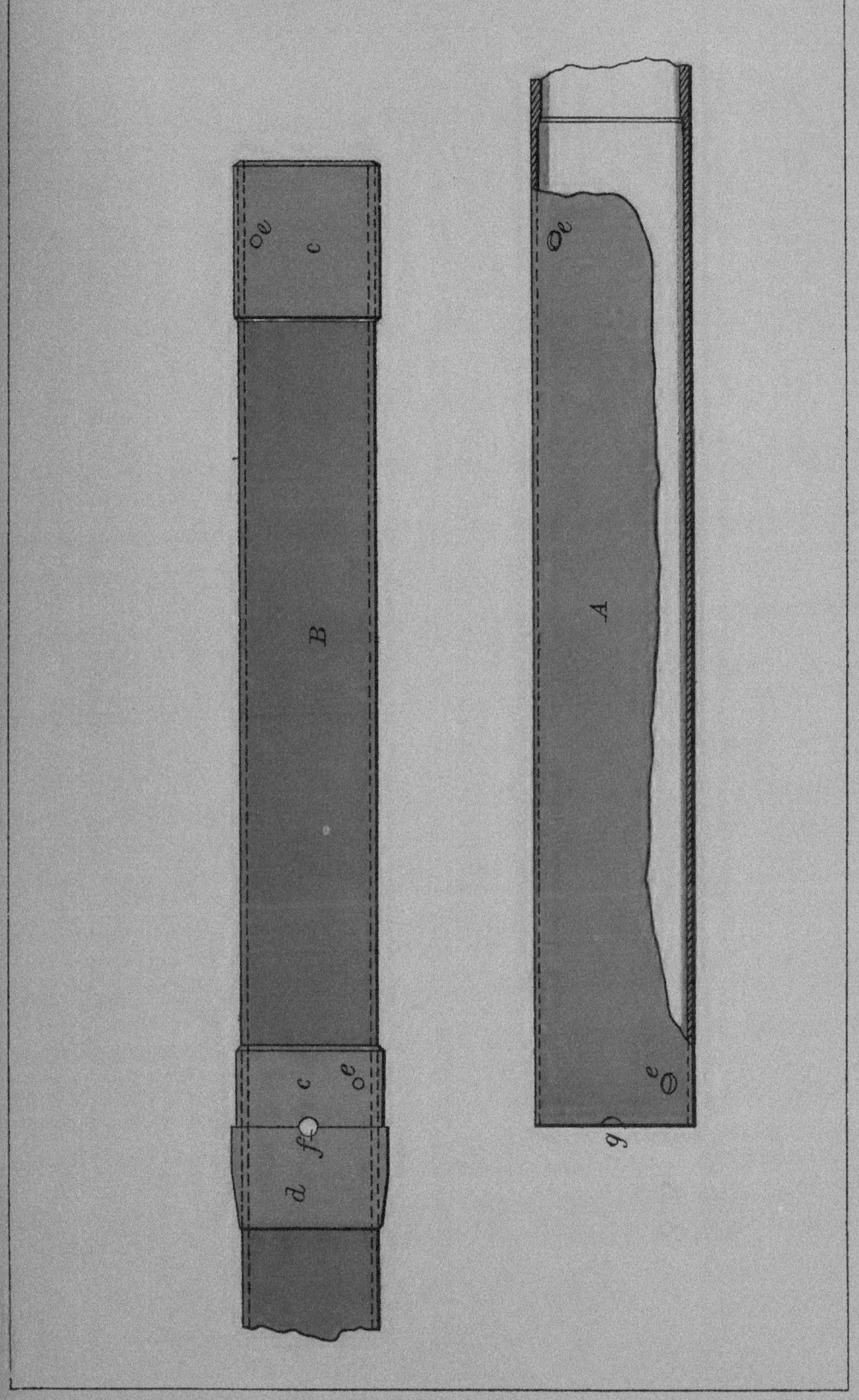

PLATE VIII.

Fig. 1, Detonator.

A copper case.
B plug.
c, c detonator-legs.
D bridge.
F gun-cotton priming.
H fulminate of mercury.

Fig. 2, Detonator Block.

A block.
B " cover.
C, C detonators.
D, D tin box.

PLATE VIII.

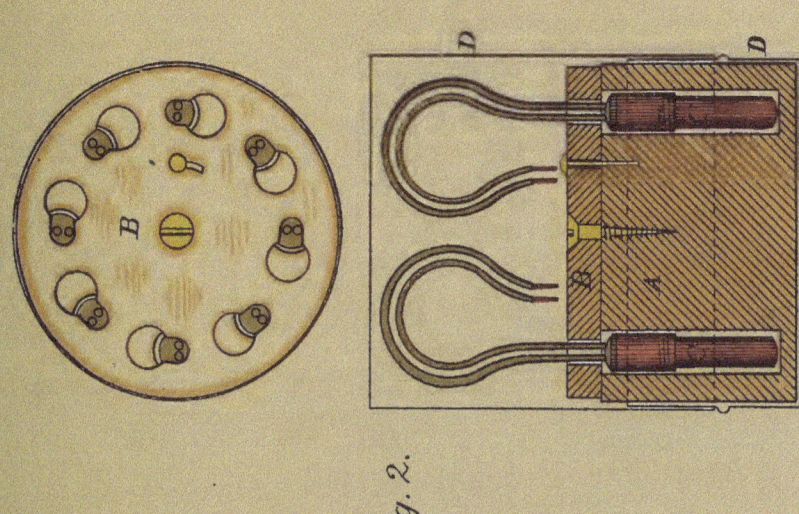

Fig. 2.

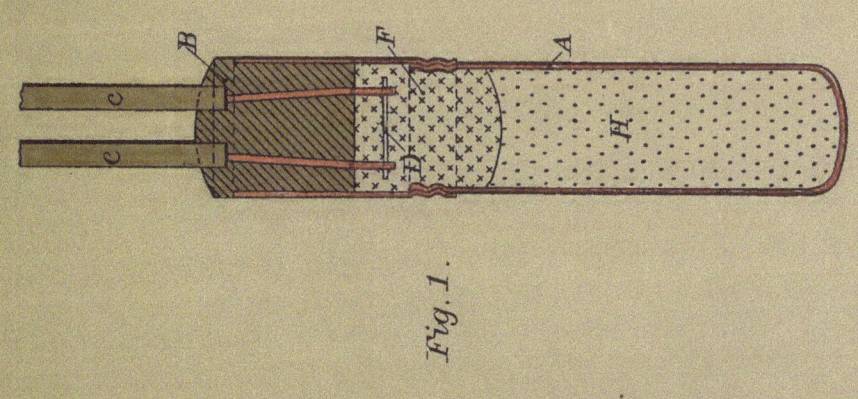

Fig. 1.

PLATE IX.

Fig. 1, Permanent Wires.

A, A electric switches (on bulwarks under bridge).
B, B forward terminals.
C, C after   "
D, D forward permanent wires.
E, E after   "   "
G, G permanent wires leading from bridge to lower binding-posts of electric switches.
H, H wires leading from bridge to common-return terminals, below switches.
K terminal on bridge for wires H, H.
L, L "   "   "   "   " G, G.
X firing-battery connected to terminals on bridge.

Fig. 2, Connections with Firing-key of "A" Machine.

B, B terminals of firing-key.
T, T "   "   "
Key "T" test key.
Key "F" firing key.
M, M wires to terminals L, L on bridge. (Fig. 1.)
N wire to terminal K on bridge (common return). (Fig. 1.)
O, O machine-connecting wires.

Fig. 3, Connections with Firing-battery.

B, B terminals of battery.
M, M wires to terminals L, L on bridge. (Fig. 1.)
N wire to terminal K on bridge (common return). (Fig. 1.)
H hand-firing key.

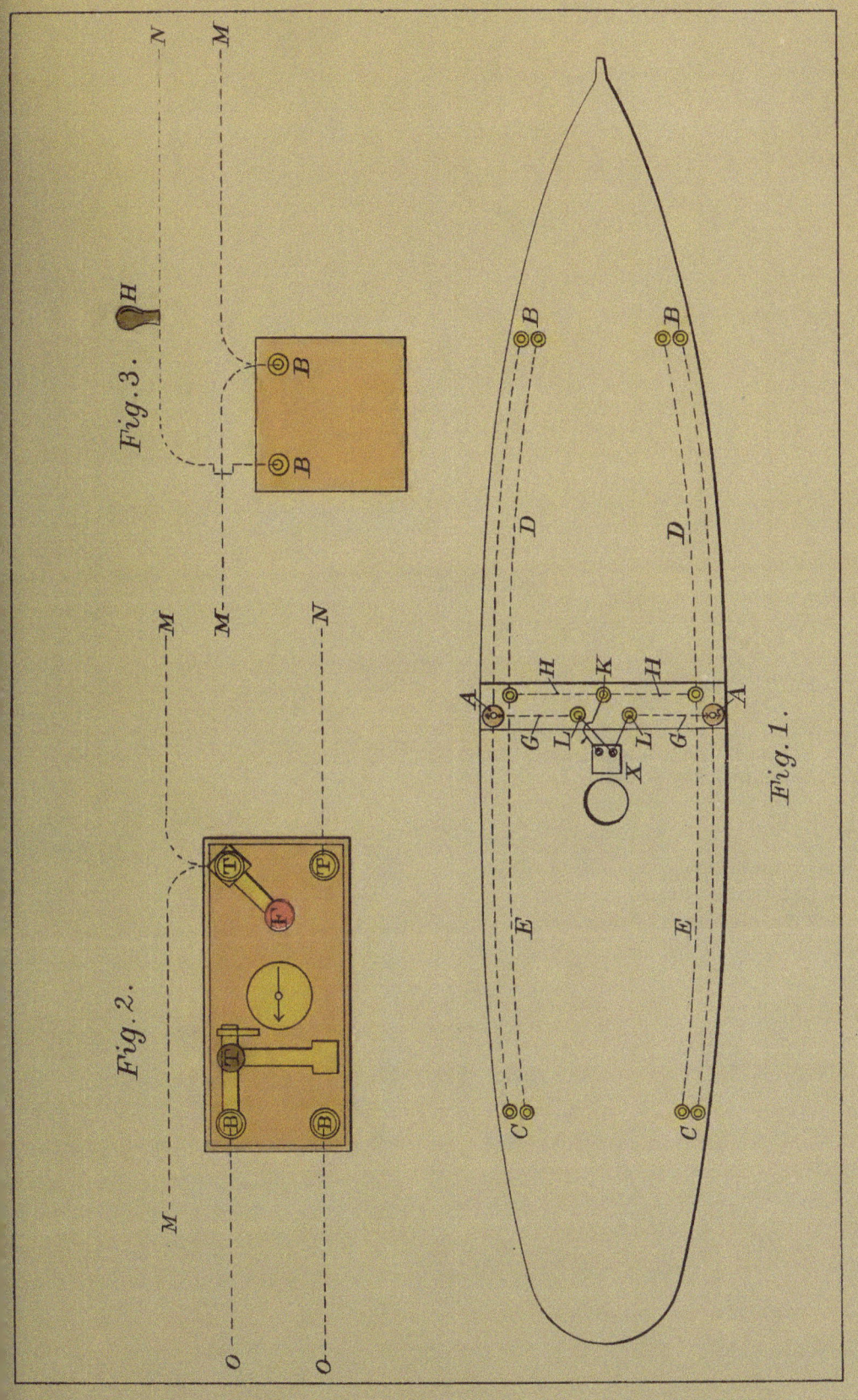

PLATE IX.

PLATE X.

Fig. 1, Electric Switch.

A permanent wire to forward torpedo.
B   "   " " after   "
C, C   "   " common return.
D wire to battery or firing-key of machine.
E commutator of switch.

Fig. 2, Terminal.

H binding-screw.
I permanent wire.
w wire temporarily connected.

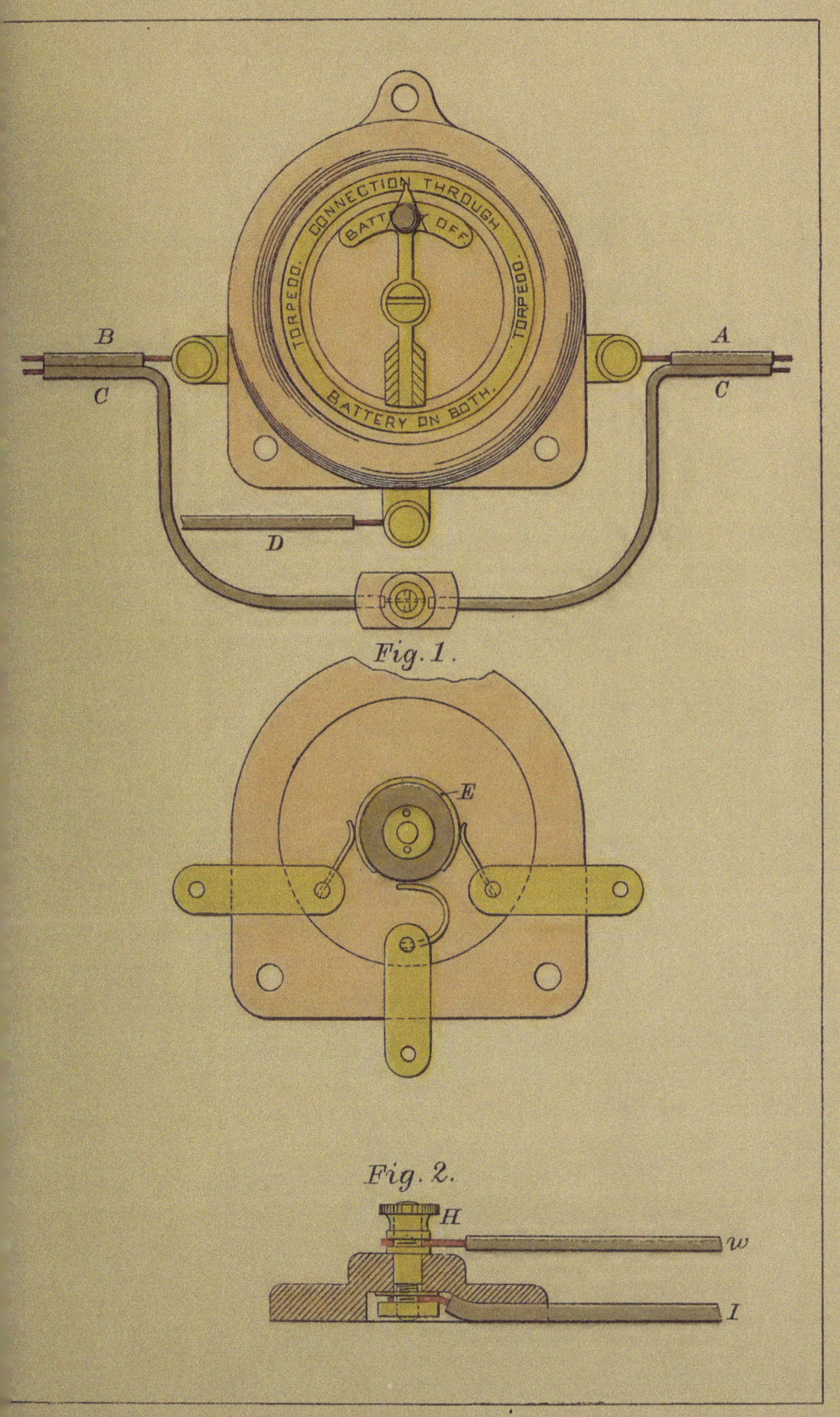

PLATE X.

PLATE XI.

Heel-fittings for Ship's Spar.

a   ship's spar.
b   thrust-plate (30″ diameter).
c   eyebolt through thrust-plate and ship's side.
d   heel-bolt.

PLATE XI.

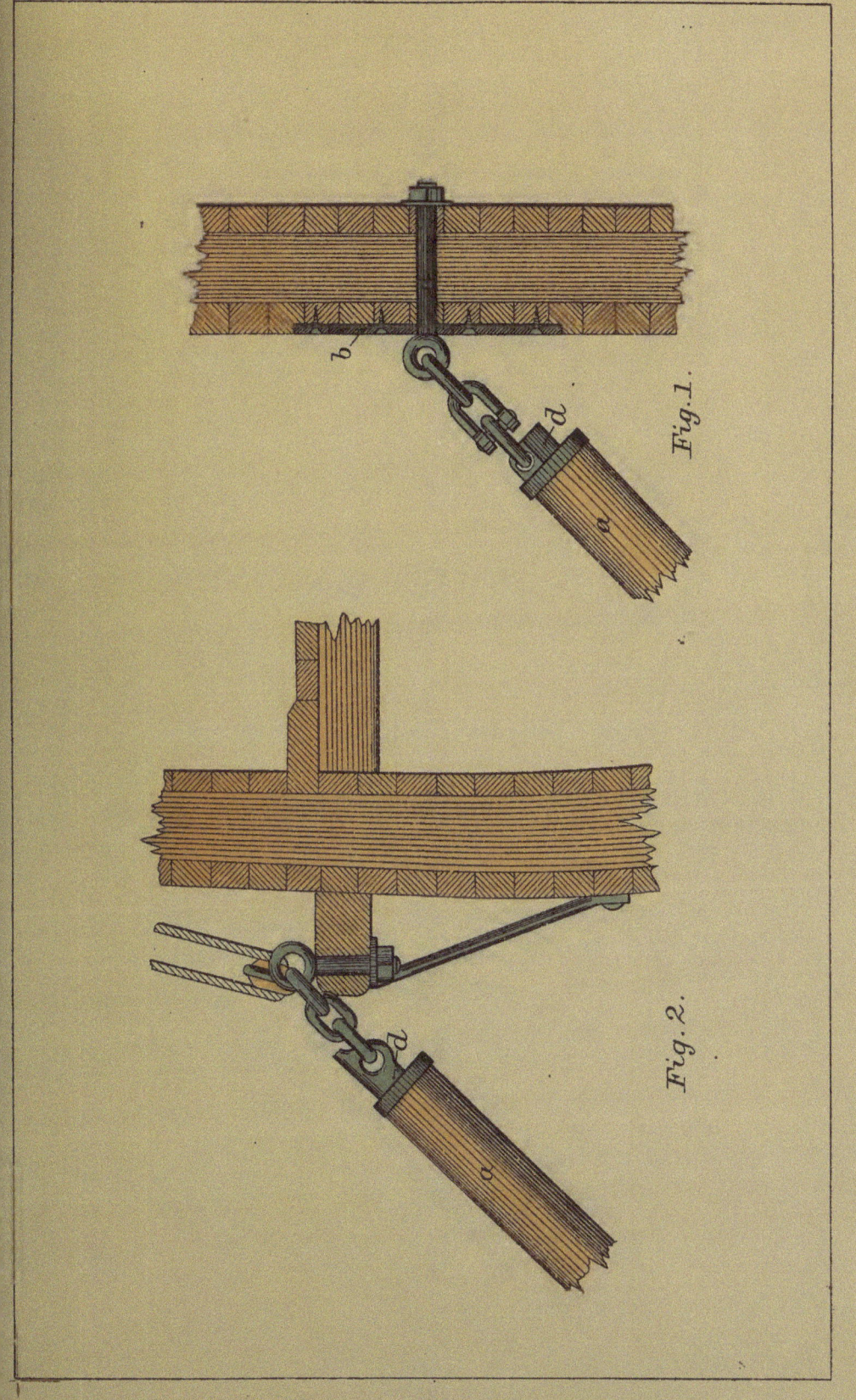

PLATE XII.

Ship's Spar Fittings.

a ship's spar.
b topping lift.
c forward guy.
d after   "
e span for topping lift (16′ long).
f   "   " forward guy (16′ long).
x, x, x, x bands on spar (5′ apart).

PLATE XII.

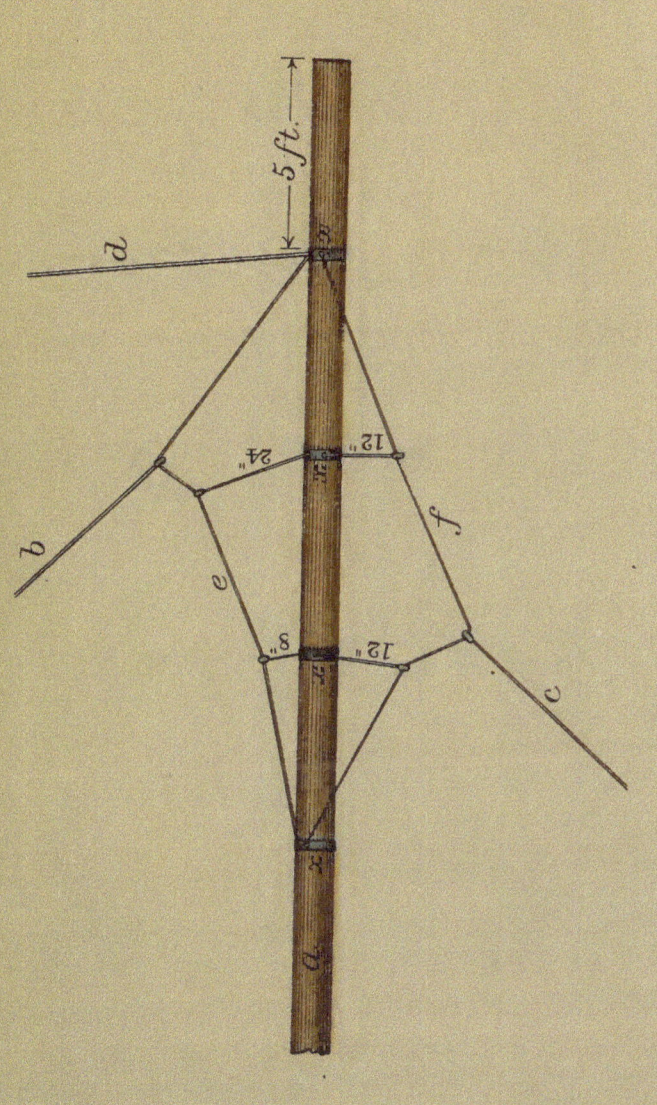

PLATE XIII.

Battery Cell.

a okonite jar.
b, b zinc cylinder.
c platinum plate.
d muslin bag filled with crushed carbon.
e ebonite disc.
f " plug.
g sal-ammoniac solution.
h positive terminal.
i negative "
k rubber cover.
r rubber ring.

PLATE XIII.

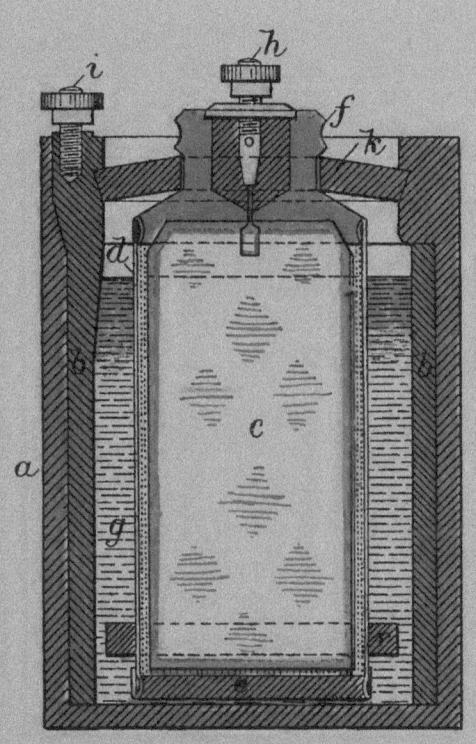

PLATE XIV.

Battery Tester.

a, a battery terminals.
b   "   tester.
c fuze-bridge in tester.

PLATE XIV.

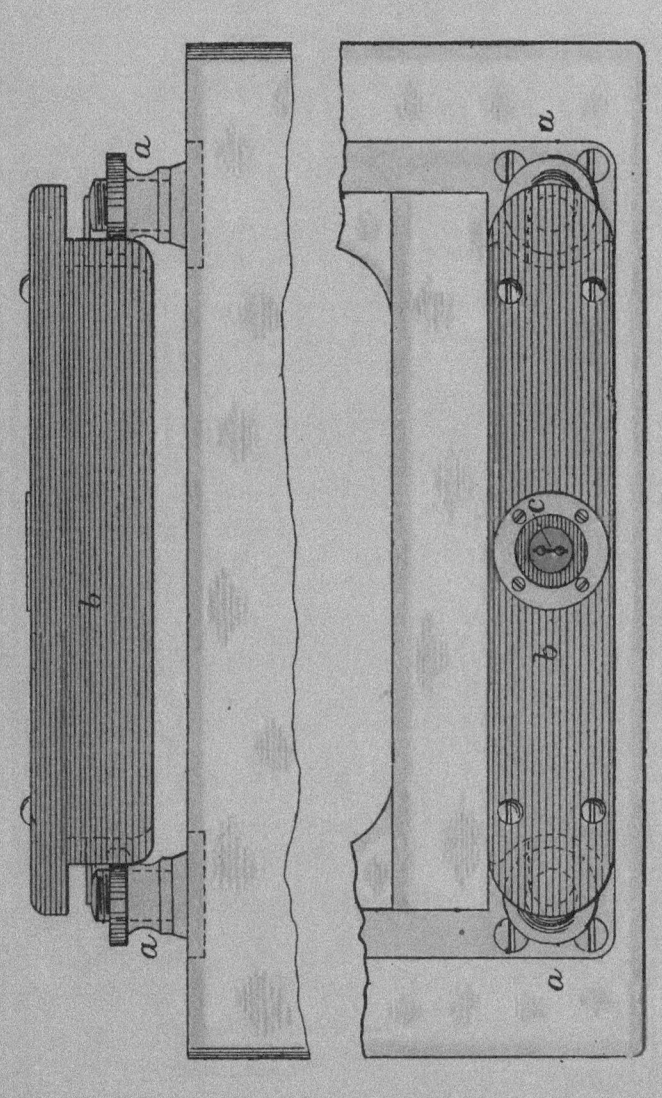

PLATE XV.

Fig. 1, Hand-firing Key. — Pattern B.

a, a hickory pieces.
c, c contact studs.
L, L leading-wires.
d rubber cot.
e safety-pin with hole for laniard.
f eye-bolt for laniard.

Fig. 2, Diagram Showing Hand-firing Key in Circuit.

B battery.
H hand-firing key.
w, w leading-wires.

PLATE XV.

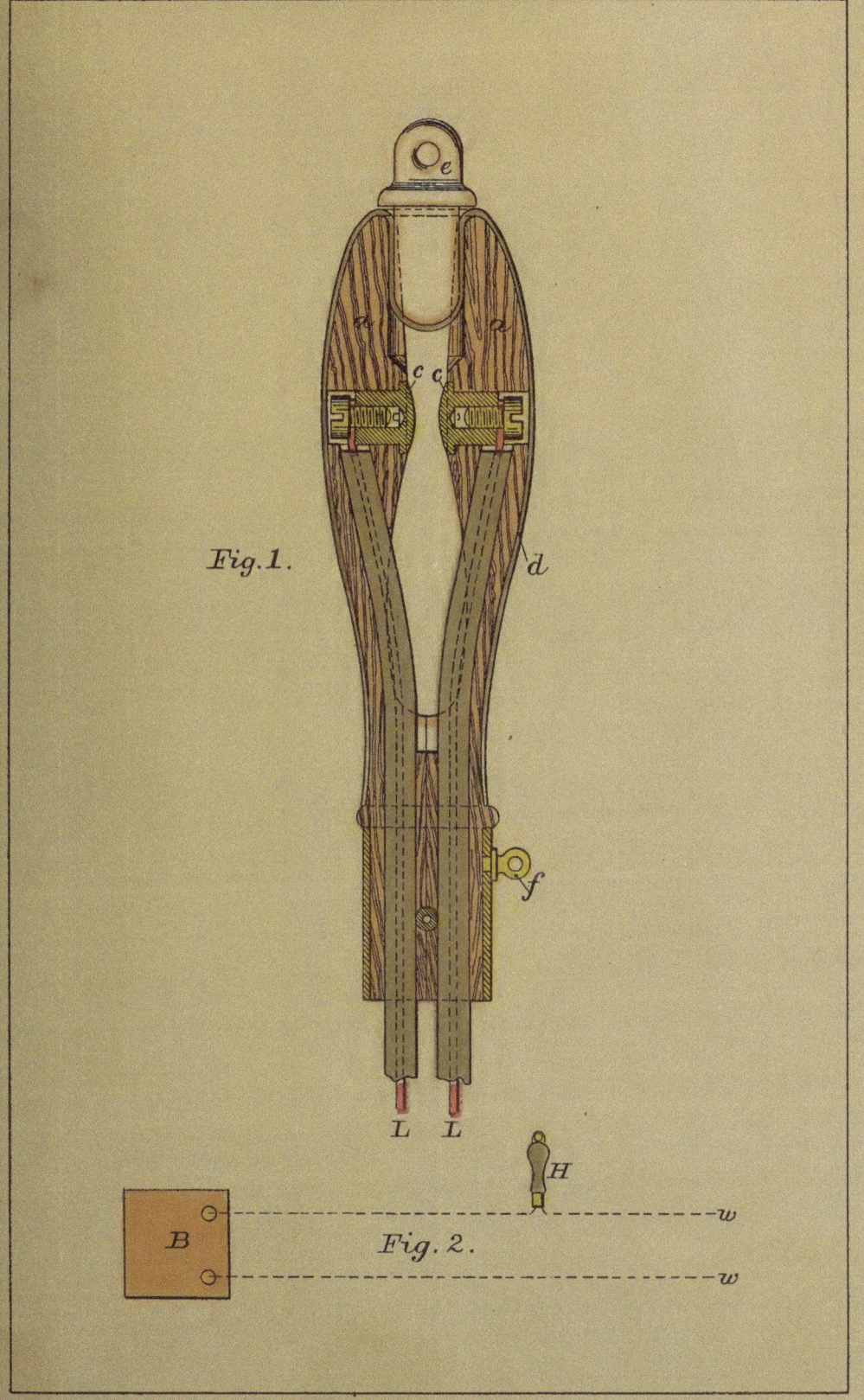

PLATE XVI.

Fig. 1, "A" Machine and Firing-key Connected.

A "A" machine.
C firing-key.
B, B terminals of firing-key.
T, T "   "   "
Key "T" test key.
 "   "F" firing-key.
O machine-connecting wires.
w, w wires to torpedo.

Fig. 2, "C" Machine Connected.

D "C" machine.
C firing-key (in the machine).
Key "T" test key.
 "   "F" firing-key.
w, w wires to torpedo.

PLATE XVI.

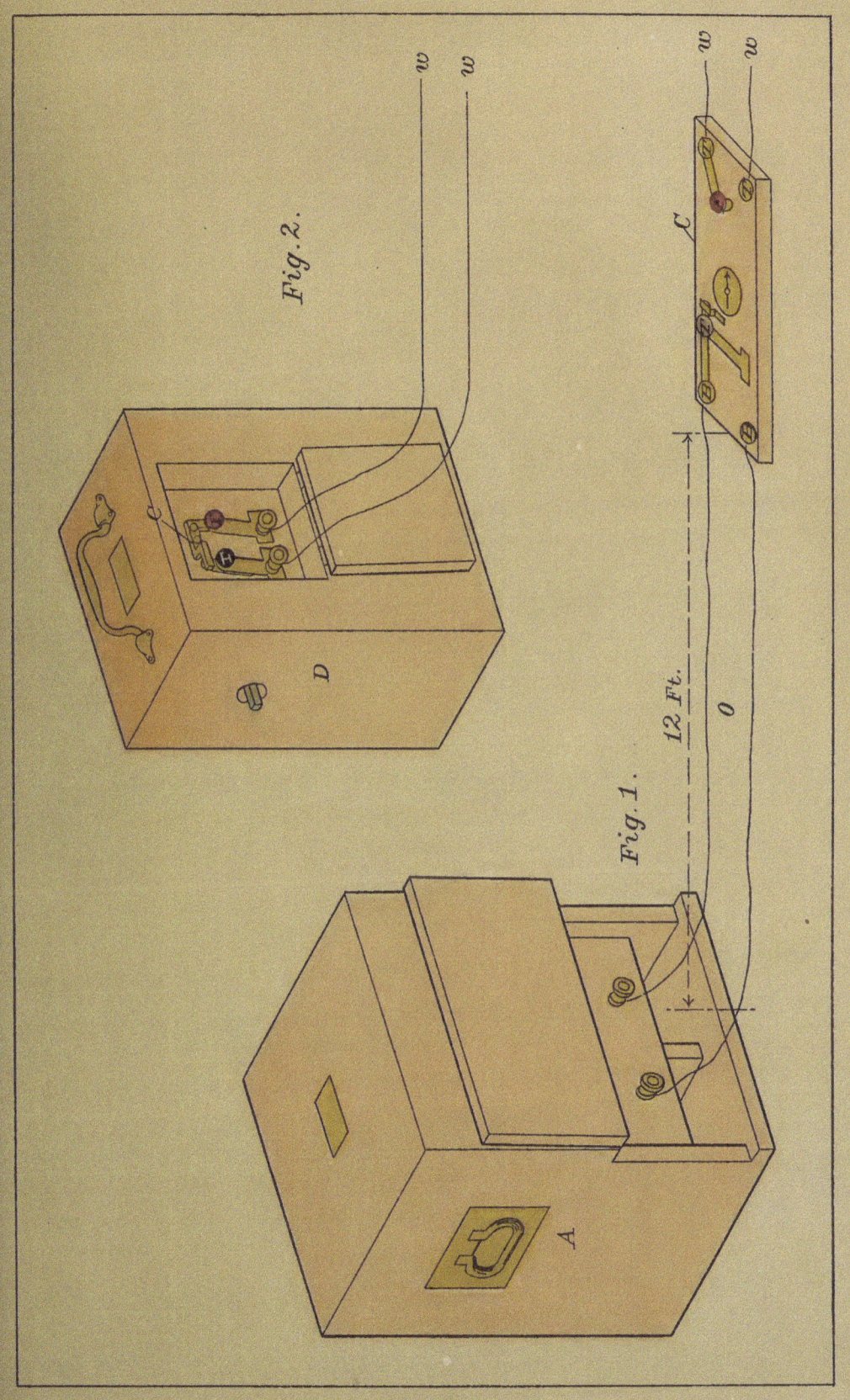

PLATE XVII.

Fig. 1, firing-key, short circuit.
" 2,   "   testing circuit.
" 3,   "   firing circuit.
O, O machine-connecting wires.
w, w wires to torpedo.
B, B terminals of firing-key.
T, T "   "   "
Key "T" test key.
Key "F" firing-key.

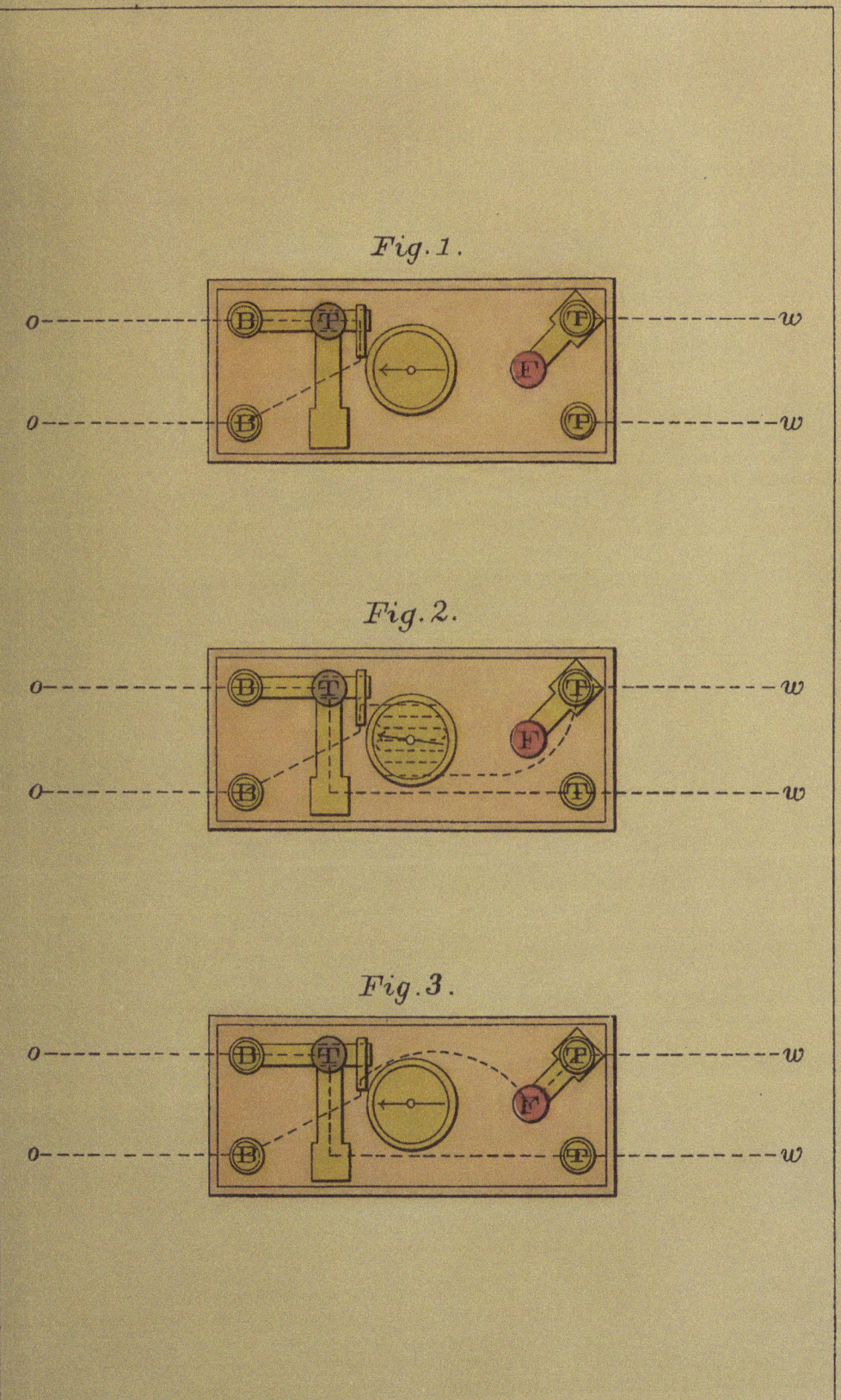

PLATE XVIII.

STEAM-DRIER.

PLATE XVIII.

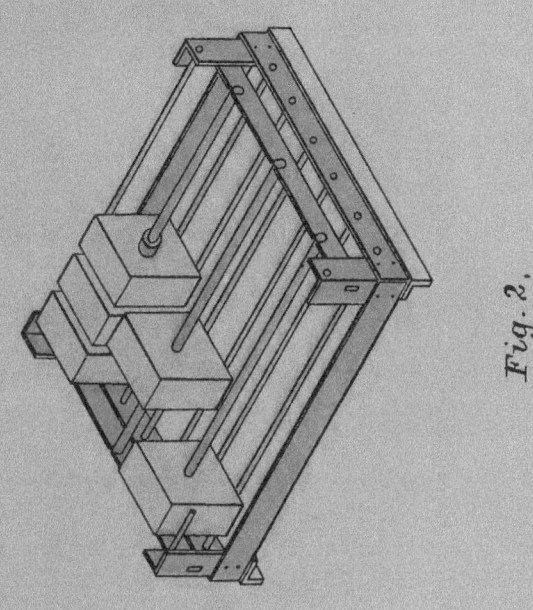

Fig. 2.

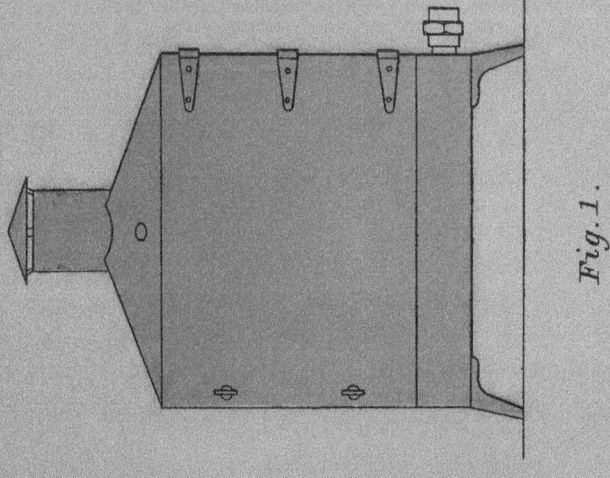

Fig. 1.

www.ingramcontent.com/pod-product-compliance
Lightning Source LLC
Chambersburg PA
CBHW062132160426
43191CB00013B/2275